First published by UAV4GEO 2026

No LLMs were used in the writing of this book.

Third edition

Cover art by Piero Toffanin

Made using free and open source software (Pandoc, LaTeX, Calibre, Inkscape, Blender, GIMP)

"Empowerment of individuals is a key part of what makes open source work, since in the end, innovations tend to come from small groups, not from large, structured efforts."

- *Tim O'Reilly*

Preface

> "If you're wondering who's in charge of writing documentation, you are."
> *-Piero Toffanin*

I never thought I'd eventually end up writing a book. I made my first code contribution to open source drone mapping software in 2016, after buying a drone and discovering that software can automatically turn 2D images into 3D models and maps. At the time, an open source project called OpenDroneMap, from which earlier editions of this book are named, was one of the few open source programs that I could manage to get up and running. However, the program was difficult to use and worked only from the command line. So over a few days I contributed a rough user interface for it. That interface later evolved into the NodeODM (now NodeODX) project. People noticed, loved it and asked for more. So that was the start of WebODM. My involvement stepped up once I started diving into the processing engine's internals and making some major contributions there along the way. At the time the program was changing so rapidly that even writing some simple documentation seemed like an impossible task. It would be obsolete in a few months, so why bother?

Today the software continues to be actively developed, but it has stabilized a lot, making the task of documenting it not only possible, but necessary.

Three years have passed since I wrote the second edition (and seven years since the first). I wasn't yet fully ready to write another edition. However, that changed quickly on April 6th 2026, when WebODM decoupled from its historical home at OpenDroneMap[1]. Due to more than 10 years of shared history between the two projects, I knew that this split meant I would have to start writing an updated edition soon.

And so WebODM: The Missing Guide was born.

I decided to offer it as a book and not as an online resource for several reasons:

- A book has a more discursive format and allows the information to be presented in a more linear fashion.
- The project already has an online reference documentation and I didn't want to rewrite the work others have already made. This book does not replace the online documentation, it complements it.
- It gives people an opportunity to financially support the project.

I'm aware that for some people buying a book might not be an option. Reasons can range from financial hardship to the inability of making purchases with a credit card. To mitigate this problem, I have setup a link on the book's website at webodmbook.com where people can apply for a free or discounted copy. Furthermore, if you purchased this book and you know somebody who is unable to get it, please feel free to forward them your copy (just please don't share it on a public site).

As soon as a fourth edition of the book is written, I pledge to release this book for everyone to download freely. The first and second editions of the book are also available for free at webodmbook.com/1 and webodmbook.com/2.

I have tried my best to write in a style that a complete novice could understand, while keeping it technical enough for advanced users to gain valuable insights. I have favored simplicity over correctness when discussing concepts, knowing that scholarly readers will know how to recognize the shortcomings of my descriptions and where to lookup the more formal definitions.

[1] WebODM has officially decoupled from OpenDroneMap: webodm.org/blog/announcement/

Preface

I'm not a professional writer and English is not my first language, so I hope the reader will forgive me for the occasional awkwardness in sentence structures or a misspelling that might have been missed during review.

I believe that constructive criticism is a key component to learning and improving. How was the book? What could be improved for the next edition? What was not clear? If you have feedback or any other comment in general, please feel free to drop me a note: pt@uav4geo.com.

Enjoy the book!

-Piero

Acknowledgements

This book would not have existed without the amazing WebODM community. I'm especially grateful to those that have purchased previous editions of this book, as without their support I don't think I would have found the motivation to write another edition.

I'm also profoundly grateful to my wife, Danielle, for her unwavering support and for accommodating the late night schedules this work required.

Finally, I'd like to thank my dad, Paolo, who introduced me at age nine to BASIC and unintentionally ignited my passion for software. I'm not sure WebODM, or this book, would exist today without him.

Thank You

Contents

Part I.

Introduction

Why WebODM?

> "What is the difference between WebODM and other software?"

I would be tempted to list the features of the software, how it's based on open standards, why thousands of organizations have chosen it as their preferred aerial data processing solution, why it scales horizontally, and *blah blah blah*.

However, WebODM software is not unique in functionality. At the time of writing (mid 2026) there are dozens of photogrammetry solutions that can deliver comparable results.

What makes the software unique, is that it offers people a choice. Prior to its creation people were mostly confined to the lands of proprietary, black-box systems. If you wished to unlock the insights of aerial data, brought to us by the recent availability of inexpensive UAVs (Unmanned Aerial Vehicles), you had no choice. Pay up, get locked-in and trust that the results are correct.

By distributing WebODM software under free and open source licenses, we have given people the ability to use, modify, examine, distribute and sell the software under very permissive terms. We have given people a choice.

Philosophical reasons aside, most users do not care about software freedom as much as they care about free pizza, so I'm excited to tell you that WebODM software can be installed at no cost on all the computers you like and scale to thousands of clusters without licensing costs, with an active community of thousands of users and organizations, all while the project receives love from different organizations that fund and benefit from its development since 2016. We offer more features than any other open source software in the field, are growing at steady pace and have plans to take over the world when the autonomous robot apocalypse arrives!

What You Can Do With WebODM

While the history and focus of the program is centered around processing aerial imagery, it's not limited to that. The application can be used to perform photogrammetry tasks in many other fields such as archaeology and architecture. Indoor scanning and modeling with the use of a classic hand-held camera, or even a phone, is also supported.

Indoor 3D model processed with WebODM, cropped in Blender

However, the software really shines when it comes to aerial imagery. By aerial imagery I mean pictures taken from UAVs, planes, kites or balloons. The software can generate georeferenced point clouds, 3D models, digital elevation models and maps, using Ground Control Points (GCPs) for better accuracy or via embedded GPS/RTK information. The program can be installed on a local machine or on cloud servers such as those provided by Amazon Web Services (AWS) or Microsoft Azure. Its internal photogrammetry engine, ODX, can be used from the command line as a standalone module. Most capabilities are exposed via Application Programming Interfaces (APIs) that can be used from the Python programming language via a dedicated Software Development Kit (SDK) or with other programming languages. The software can be integrated into new and existing platforms and allows organizations to scale their processing capabilities as needed.

Today companies, government entities, professionals and hobbyists alike use some or all parts of the WebODM's software ecosystem to perform a variety of tasks, including:

- Monitoring crops in agriculture.
- Mapping land areas.
- Performing hydrological analysis.
- Reporting construction progress.
- Classifying and counting trees.
- Analyzing stockpile volumes.
- Documenting car crashes.
- Inspecting roofs and cell towers.
- Documenting proof of work completion.
- Archeological artifact scanning.
- Improving OpenStreetMap.
- Stitching historical aerial images.
- Monitoring vehicle traffic flows.

This list is by no means exhaustive. We often encounter new ingenious ways in how people are using the software. WebODM offers a collection of solutions for collecting, processing, analyzing and displaying aerial data. Aside from the classical uses, let creativity and imagination be the limit.

The project has a website hosted on webodm.org. If you haven't looked around the website yet, I encourage you to take a peek and look over some of the gallery screenshots that have been contributed by the community. You might find inspiration for novel things to do with the software.

Becoming a Successful User

As an open source project, users can choose to download the software, read the documentation, start using it and be done. Maybe file a bug report when problems occur. We're happy when people just want to use the software and be done.

However, we recommend people join the vibrant WebODM community if they are using the software. This unlocks many benefits, such as:

- The ability to propose the addition of a missing feature.
- Becoming an expert in one or more areas of the program by helping others.
- Getting bugs that affect them personally resolved more quickly.
- Helping to steer the direction of the project.
- Participating in community events around the globe, meeting people and making new friends.

People are often hesitant to join and participate in a community, mostly because they think they have nothing worthy to contribute and time is a rare commodity.

But before going to the next chapter, I invite you to join one of the many friendly WebODM communities at webodm.org/community. Introduce yourself, tell people how you are hoping to use the software or anything else about you. That's a contribution and takes just a few minutes. After reading this book, you can also try to answer a question from a fellow user. The cycle of reciprocal help will come back to you.

Plus, you might even have some fun along the way and have a chance to meet other fellow drone mappers in the process!

Part II.

Getting Started

1. The WebODM Ecosystem

WebODM is the primary software in a wider ecosystem of applications to process, analyze and display aerial data:

- **ODX** is the photogrammetry engine, which can be used from the command line. It takes images as input and produces a variety of outputs, including point clouds, elevation models, 3D models and orthophotos.
- **NodeODX** is a light-weight API built on top of ODX. It allows users and applications to access the functions of ODX over computer networks.
- **CloudODX** is a small command line client to communicate with ODX via the NodeODX API.
- **PyODX** is a Python SDK for creating tasks via the NodeODX API. We cover it in more detail in the Automated Processing With Python chapter.
- **ClusterODX** is a load balancer for connecting together multiple NodeODX instances and is covered in the Processing Large Datasets chapter.
- **OATS** (ODX Automated Testing Suite) is a set of tools and scripts to test and analyze datasets processed with ODX.

- **CameraLib** is a Python library to perform forward and backward projection of 2D coordinates in camera space to geographic coordinates.

2. Installing The Software

I believe in a practical and incremental approach to learning. To keep things as simple as possible, we will begin with the installation and usage of WebODM, which under the hood also installs ODX and NodeODX. Installing WebODM on Windows and macOS is relatively simple, as installers are freely available to download. On Linux the installation requires some use of the command line, but not much. We'll leave the command line aside until part III, where we will cover more advanced uses that require it. By then readers will be comfortable with the core concepts of the program and the learning curve will be more gradual. Advanced users that are familiar with the installation process may wish to skip this chapter.

WebODM, ODX and NodeODX are available on all major platforms (Windows, macOS and Linux) via a program called docker. Docker is a tool to run *containers*, which are packaged copies of an entire system, its software and its dependencies. These containers run within a virtual environment. On Linux this virtual environment is available from the operating system and is very efficient. On macOS and Windows the containers run within a Virtual Machine (VM), so there's a bit of overhead, but not a lot. Once installed users do not have to worry much about docker, as it can be used as a simple tool to launch WebODM and nothing else. We dedicate an entire chapter to more advanced uses of docker in the Docker Essentials chapter.

We often get asked why we use docker, since it tends to be a pain to install and configure on platforms other than Linux. ODX is a complex software and relies on many dependencies. Docker makes it simple to package and distribute the software and its dependencies in a way that is consistent across platforms (Windows, Mac and Linux).

It should be noted that this is not the only way to run WebODM. On Windows the software can run natively (without docker) and a one-click installer is available that makes installation a breeze. On macOS, while docker is still required, there's also an installer that makes the installation process much simpler.

WebODM used to have a reputation among many people of being a difficult software to install. As of 2026, I believe this is no longer the case.

One final note about docker: at the time of writing Docker Desktop requires a license if you are a company with more than 250 employees or have more than $10 million USD in annual revenue. I suspect most people reading this book do not run a company of this size, but be aware of this licensing requirement if you use docker.

Hardware Requirements

The bare minimum requirements for running the software are:

- 64bit CPU manufactured on or after 2010
- 20 GB of disk space
- 4 GB RAM

No more than 100-200 images can be processed with these specifications (the software will run out of memory). Recommended requirements are:

- Latest generation CPU

- 100 GB of disk space
- 16 GB RAM

Which will allow for a few hundred images to be processed without too many issues. A CPU with more cores will allow for faster processing. A (single) NVIDIA GPU can also be used for speeding some parts of processing. For processing more images, add more disk space and RAM linearly to the number of images you need to process.

Installing on Windows

To run WebODM you need at least Windows 10. Previous versions of Windows are not supported.

To get started, download and run the latest Windows Installer from webodm.org/download.

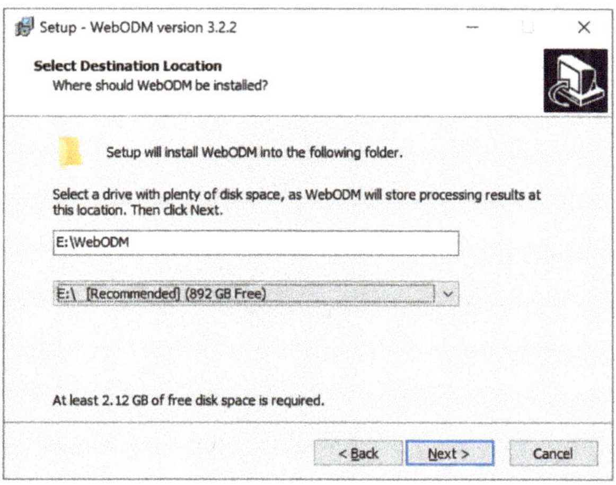

Choose a drive with plenty of disk space

At the first startup of the application, you might be asked by your firewall to allow communication between the NodeODX and WebODM processes. Make sure to answer yes to that question.

Installing on macOS

Most modern (post 2013) Mac computers running macOS Big Sur 11 or higher can run WebODM. If your computer cannot run macOS Big Sur 11, the computer is too old :(

Step 1. Install WebODM

To get started, download and run the latest macOS Installer from webodm.org/download.

Through the installation process you will be asked to type your password in order to install Docker. After Docker has been installed, the installer will download WebODM and run the necessary docker commands to get the program started.

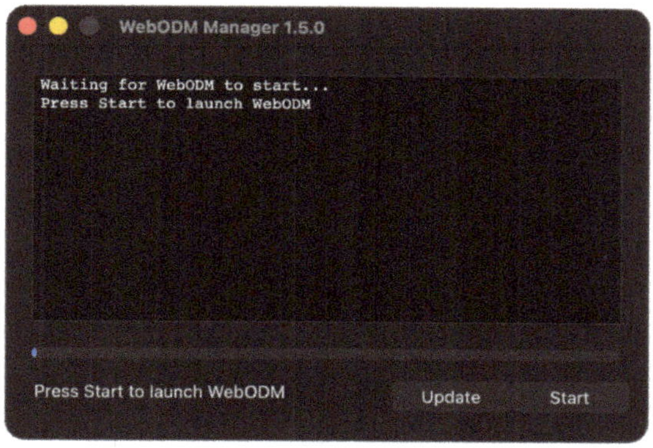

You can start, stop and update WebODM from the WebODM Manager

At the end of the process, your browser should automatically open to http://localhost:8000, displaying WebODM's welcome page. If not, you can open it manually.

You will be greeted with a welcome message and will be asked to create the first user.

After installation you should find an icon that looks like a whale in the task bar.

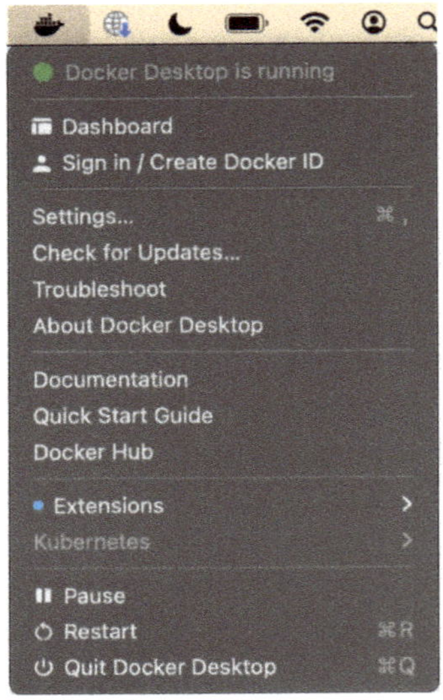

Docker Tray on macOS

That's the Docker Desktop application.

Step 2. Check Memory and CPU Allocation

Docker on macOS works by running a VM in the background (think of it as a sort of computer emulator). This VM has a certain amount of memory allocated and WebODM can only use as much memory as it's allocated.

1. Right click the whale icon from the task bar and click **Settings...**
2. Select the **Resources** tab.
3. Adjust the CPUs slider to use half of all available CPUs and the memory to use 50-70% of all available memory.
4. Press **Apply & Restart**.

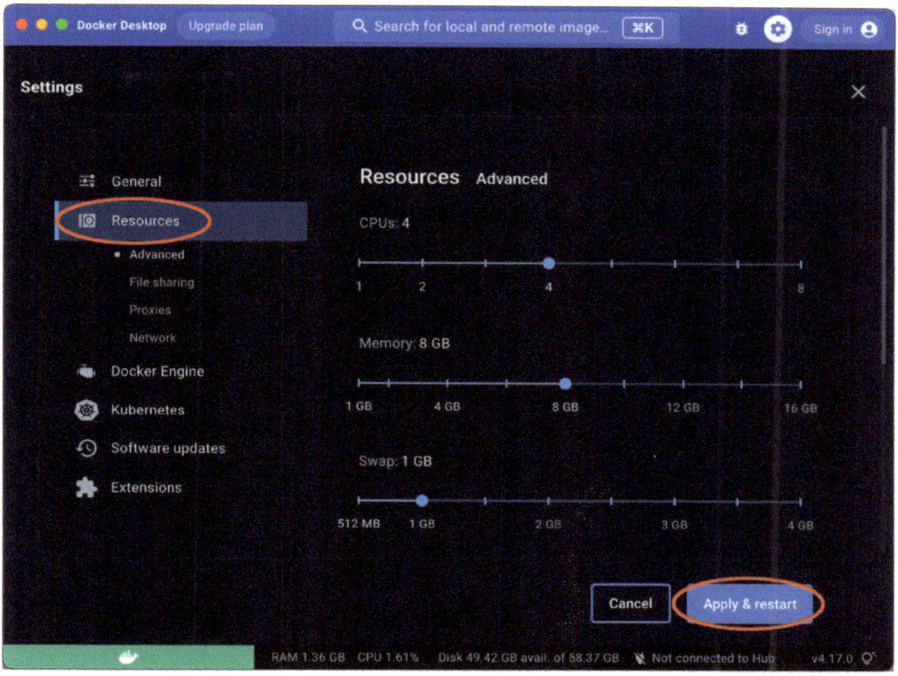

Docker Settings

Installing on Linux

WebODM can run on any Linux distribution that supports docker. According to docker's documentation website[1] the officially supported distributions are CentOS, Debian, Ubuntu and Fedora, with static binaries available for others (I use Arch Linux quite successfully). If you have to pick a distribution solely for running WebODM, Ubuntu is the recommended one.

[1]Docker Documentation: docs.docker.com/install/

Step 1. Install Requirements

You'll need to install:

1. Docker
2. Git

We cannot possibly cover the installation process for every Linux distribution out there, so we'll limit the instructions to those that are distributions officially supported by docker. In all cases it's just a matter of opening a terminal prompt and typing a few commands.

Install on Ubuntu / Debian

Commands to type:

```
$ sudo apt update
$ curl -fsSL https://get.docker.com -o get-docker.sh
$ sh get-docker.sh
```

Install on CentOS / RHEL

Commands to type:

```
$ curl -fsSL https://get.docker.com -o get-docker.sh
$ sh get-docker.sh
$ sudo yum -y install git
```

Install on Fedora

Commands to type:

```
$ curl -fsSL https://get.docker.com -o get-docker.sh
$ sh get-docker.sh
$ sudo dnf install git
```

Install on Arch

Commands to type:

```
$ sudo pacman -Sy docker git
```

Step 2. Download and Launch WebODM

From a terminal type:

```
$ git clone https://github.com/WebODM/WebODM
$ cd WebODM
$ ./webodm.sh start
```

Then open a web browser and navigate to http://localhost:8000

You will be greeted with a welcome message and will be asked to create the first user.

Basic Linux Commands

On Linux, if you want to stop WebODM, you can press **CTRL+C** or use the following command:

```
$ ./webodm.sh stop
```

There are several other commands you can use, along with different parameters. Parameters passed to the ./webodm.sh command and are typically prefixed with two dashes. The `--port` parameter for example instructs WebODM to use a different network port:

Run WebODM on port 80 instead of 8000

```
$ ./webodm.sh restart --port 80
```

Other useful commands are listed below:

Command	Action
`$ ./webodm.sh restart`	Restart WebODM (useful if things get stuck)
`$ ./webodm.sh resetadminpassword newpass`	Reset the admin user's password if you forgot it
`$ ./webodm.sh update`	Update everything to the latest version
`$ ./webodm.sh restart --media-dir /path/`	Store processing results in the specified folder instead of the default location (inside docker)
`./webodm.sh --help`	See more command line options

For general maintenance tasks, including backups and troubleshooting, WebODM's documentation website has the most up-to-date instructions[2] and it's well worth a read. The community directory[3] is also a great place to find communities to ask for help if you get stuck during any of the installation steps and for general questions.

Hello, WebODM!

Take some time to familiarize yourself with the web interface and explore its various menus.

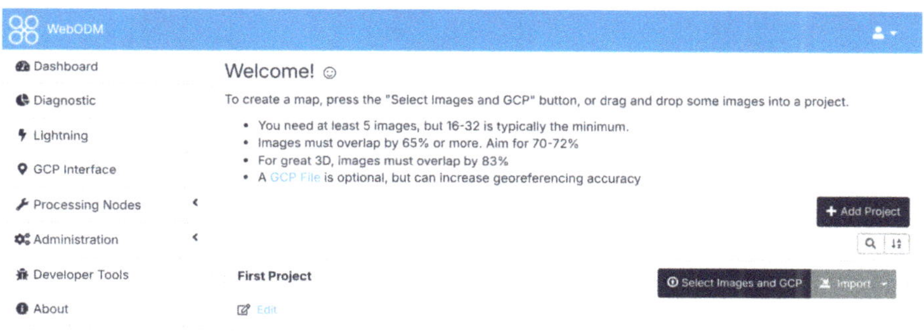

WebODM dashboard

Notice that under the **Processing Nodes** menu there's a *node-odx-1* node already configured for you to use. This is a NodeODX node and has been created automatically by WebODM. This node is running on the same machine as WebODM. In *The Command Line* chapter we will explore how to add new nodes, even from different machines.

[2]WebODM Documentation: docs.webodm.org
[3]WebODM Community: webodm.org/community

Now it's time to process some data.

3. Processing Datasets

If you own a drone, I recommend trying to process images you've collected: it's more gratifying than using somebody else's. WebODM does not (yet) have a flight planner or a flight controller application, but there are many freely available such as DJI GS Pro[1] or QGroundControl[2] that can help you capture a dataset. For advice on data collection, also check the Flying Tips chapter. If you need some sample data, there are many freely available datasets you can download from webodm.org/datasets.

Dataset Size

Depending on the amount of RAM available on your computer, you might want to choose a small dataset (less than 100 images) to start with. Memory requirements for processing are mostly proportional to the number of images and there are no reliable benchmarks at the time of writing that can tell you exactly how much memory you will need ahead of time. So the best way is to start small and gradually increase. Some task options can also affect memory requirements. Task options are covered in detail in the Task Options in Depth chapter.

[1] DJI GS Pro: dji.com/ground-station-pro
[2] QGroundControl: qgroundcontrol.com

File Requirements

The software can process any of the following:

- Color images (JPEG, TIFF, PNG, DNG, NEF, RAW, JXL).
- Multispectral and thermal images (TIFF).
- Video files (MP4, MOV, LRV, TS).

Color images can come from different cameras and can be taken at different angles. Most drone and phone cameras will also add geolocation information in the files in the form of Exchangeable Image File Format (EXIF) tags. EXIF tags are small pieces of information embedded within an image, which usually include the geographical location of where a picture was taken. Geolocation information is required to produce georeferenced orthophotos and elevation models, but it is not required for creating point clouds and 3D models. You can use pictures that have no geolocation information, but the results will not be georeferenced and they will not be usable for making measurements.

If you have pictures with no geolocation information, you can either use a Ground Control Point (GCP) file or create a Geolocation (GEO) file. GCPs and GEO files are covered in more detail in the Ground Control Points and Geolocation Files chapters.

You can use GIMP[3] to check whether your images have geolocation information. If you open an image with GIMP, press the **Image** menu, then go to **Metadata — View Metadata**. From the **EXIF** tab you should be able to find the GPSAltitude, GPSLatitude and GPSLongitude tags. If you don't see them, the image does not have geolocation information.

Video files are processed by extracting image frames at regular intervals, then processing is performed on the extracted color images.

[3]GIMP: gimp.org

We will cover multispectral images, which include thermal images, in the Multispectral Datasets chapter.

Process Tasks

Press the **Select Images and GCP** button or drag and drop your images in a project. You can also press the button multiple times to add files from multiple folders.

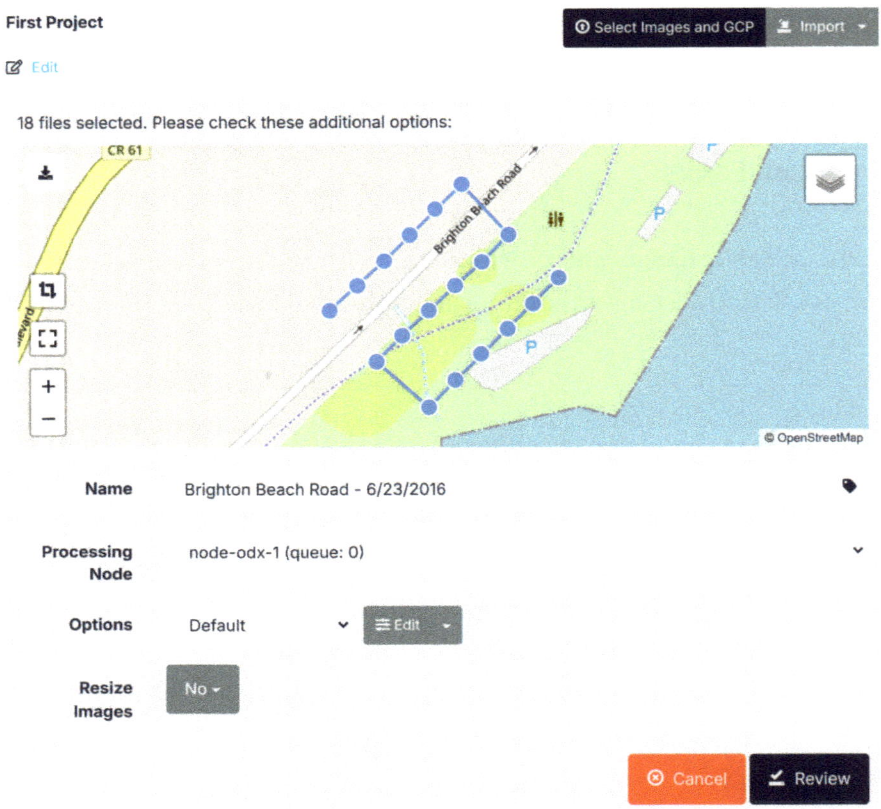

WebODM's new task panel

There are a few settings you can choose:

- **Name:** a label for the task.
- **Processing Node:** is the processing node that will process the task. **node-odx-1** is the default node that is created automatically by WebODM.

- **Options:** you can choose one from a predefined list of presets. You can hover your mouse cursor over the currently selected preset to see what options are being used. Several default presets are available, but you are encouraged to experiment and create your own presets. Pressing the button next to the preset list brings up the edit task options panel, while pressing the arrow button next to it allows you to save, edit or remove existing presets. Task options are covered in detail in the Task Options in Depth chapter. For now choose the **Default** preset.
- **Resize Images:** for reducing storage requirements, lowering memory usage and increasing processing speed, at the expense of potentially lower quality results, you can choose to resize your images prior to processing. Note that video files will not be resized.

When images have geolocation information, the map preview panel will display their locations. From this panel it's also possible to set an optional boundary, which will limit the reconstruction area.

When you are ready, press **Review** and then **Start Processing**. After processing starts:

1. Images are copied to the `app/media` folder within WebODM. Note that when using docker this folder is not accessible from your computer unless you passed the `--media-dir` parameter when starting WebODM as explained at the end of the Installing The Software chapter.
2. Images are sent to the processing node. If this seems redundant (why not copy the images directly to the processing node?) keep in mind that processing nodes can be located on remote computers.
3. A task is started. Information such as time elapsed and console output are refreshed every few seconds.

Once the task is completed the results are transferred from the processing node to WebODM.

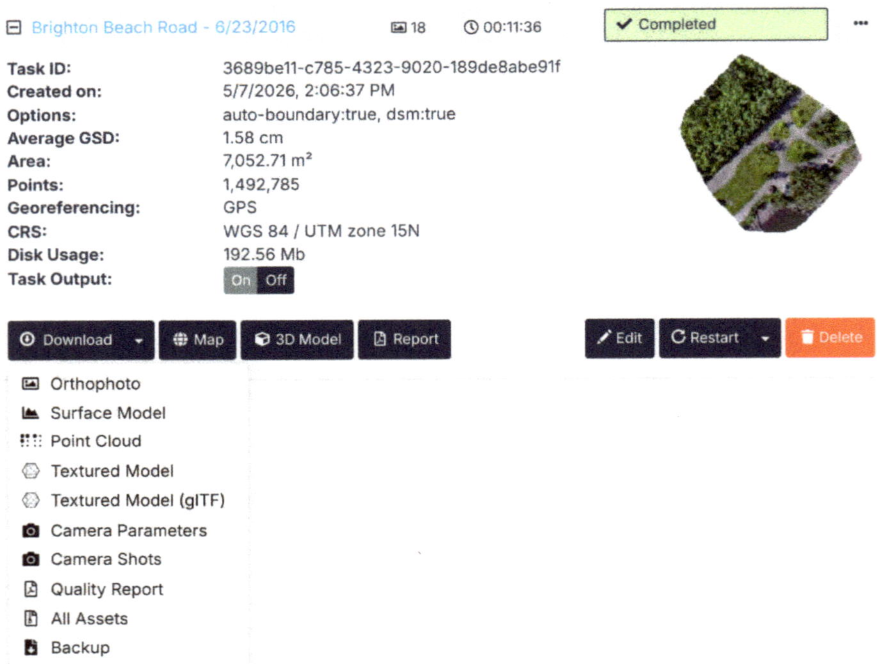

WebODM download results

Each task displays some useful information:

- **Task ID**: unique identifier.
- **Created on**: when the task was created (not when the pictures were taken).
- **Options**: a text representation of the options that were selected for processing.
- **Average GSD**: Ground Sampling Distance (GSD) is a measure of

resolution. Think of it as the real distance represented by two adjacent pixels from an aerial image. Lower GSD = Higher resolution.

- **Area**: of the rectangle enclosing the task.
- **Points**: number of points in the point cloud.
- **Georeferencing**: whether the task was georeferenced with GPS (GPS), GPS and Ground Control Points (GPS/GCP), just Ground Control Points (GCP), by alignment to another task (Alignment).
- **CRS**: name of the Coordinate Reference System in which outputs are stored.
- **Disk Usage**: amount of disk space used by all files associated with this task, including the original images.

Testing Different Task Options

It's easy and extremely fast to make copies of a task to run experiments for trying out and comparing different task options. Find the **...** button to the right of a task and click **Duplicate**. The newly duplicated options can be changed and reprocessed without affecting the original.

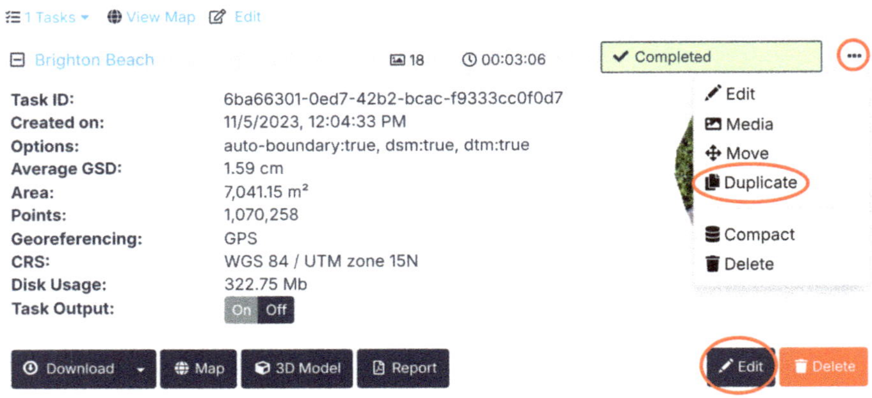

Duplicate a task, then edit

The **node-odx-1** node by default node keeps in storage the intermediate processing files of a task for 2 days. This allows WebODM to restart a task from the middle of a processing step. This is often useful for testing different task options without the need to reprocess a task from the beginning. In the Task Options in Depth chapter I give details about which options can be restarted from which step.

4. Essential Operations

Over the years WebODM has evolved from a simple processing interface to a more complete platform for displaying, sharing and analyzing aerial data. Below we will cover a (non-exhaustive) list of useful operations that can be performed after one or more datasets have been processed.

View Results

Results can be downloaded or viewed directly from one of two interfaces:

- **Map**: displays a 2D map where orthophotos and elevation models can be explored. Tools are available for generating contours, making volume measurements and more.

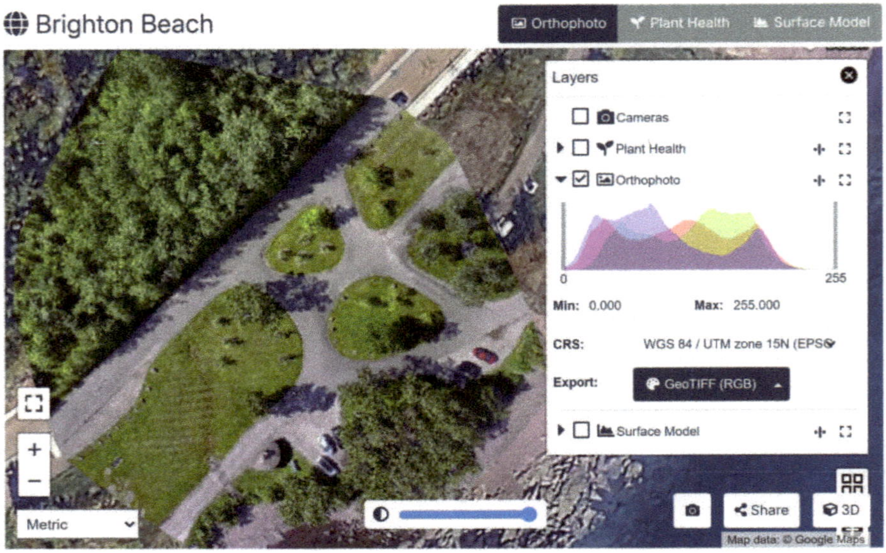

- **3D Model:** shows an interactive point cloud visualization. If a textured model is available, it can be toggled for inspection. Various tools can be used to make measurements, create elevation profiles, clip areas of the point cloud, toggle camera locations and more.

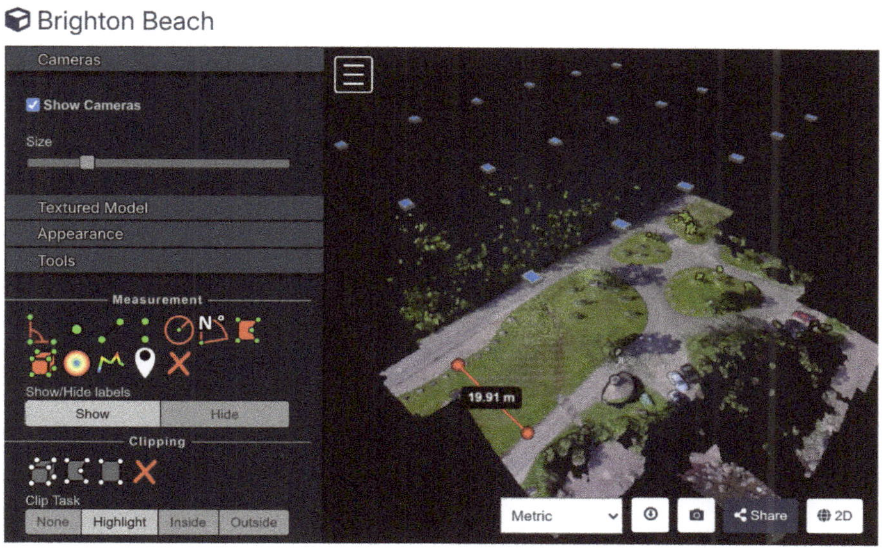

Download the Raw Assets

If you download the results by pressing the **Download — All Assets** button you will find an archive containing several files and directories:

- **entwine_pointcloud** is a representation of the point cloud that can be streamed efficiently over the web using a viewer such as potree[1].
- **odm_dem** stores the digital elevation model files.
- **odm_georeferencing** contains the dense point cloud (*odm_georeferenced_model.laz*) as well as other georeferenced files.
- **odm_orthophoto** stores the orthophoto.
- **odm_report** contains a copy of the PDF report (*report.pdf*), the same report information in machine-friendly format (*stats.json*) and a file

[1]Viewing Entwine Data: entwine.io/en/latest/quickstart.html#viewing-the-data

containing information about the images (*shots.geojson*) which can be imported in programs such as QGIS[2].

- **odm_texturing** stores the textured 3D model (*odm_textured_model_geo.obj*), which can be viewed in programs such as MeshLab[3]. A copy of the same model is available in Binary glTF format(*odm_textured_model_geo.glb*) and can be opened with a glTF Viewer[4].
- **cameras.json** has information about the sensors that were used to capture the images.
- **images.json** contains yet more information about the images.
- **log.json** is a machine-friendly copy of the task output.
- **task_output.txt** is a human-friendly copy of the task output.

Share Results With Others

From either **Map** or **3D Model** view you will find a **Share** button. Pressing this button will generate links that can be shared publicly with others. Note that the links will only work if WebODM has been installed on a server with a public IP address. If you are running WebODM on your local computer, you will not be able to share those links with others, unless you have configured the proper forwarding rules on your router/firewall. Typically if you want to share tasks with others you should install WebODM on a server.

[2]QGIS: qgis.org
[3]MeshLab: meshlab.net
[4]Don McCurdy's glTF Viewer: gltf-viewer.donmccurdy.com

Read the Quality Report

Clicking the **Report** button opens the PDF quality report, which contains a lot of useful information and that we cover in detail in the Report Analysis chapter.

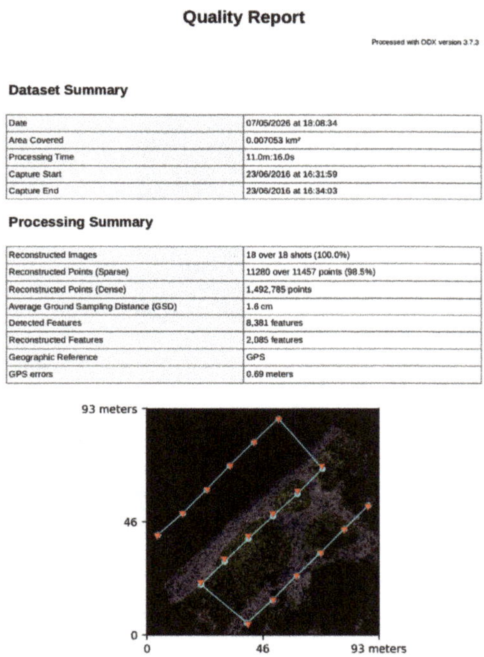

Quality Report

Processed with ODX version 3.7.3

Dataset Summary

Date	07/05/2026 at 18:08:34
Area Covered	0.007053 km²
Processing Time	11.0m:16.0s
Capture Start	23/06/2016 at 16:31:59
Capture End	23/06/2016 at 16:34:03

Processing Summary

Reconstructed Images	18 over 18 shots (100.0%)
Reconstructed Points (Sparse)	11280 over 11457 points (98.5%)
Reconstructed Points (Dense)	1,492,785 points
Average Ground Sampling Distance (GSD)	1.6 cm
Detected Features	8,381 features
Reconstructed Features	2,085 features
Geographic Reference	GPS
GPS errors	0.69 meters

First page of a PDF report

View Map Layers Side by Side

If a project contains multiple tasks, clicking the **View Map** link from the top of each project displays orthophotos and elevation models of all tasks in the project simultaneously.

You can then open the **Layers** panel and click the **Side by Side** button next to a layer to enable a slider which allows two layers to be compared side by side.

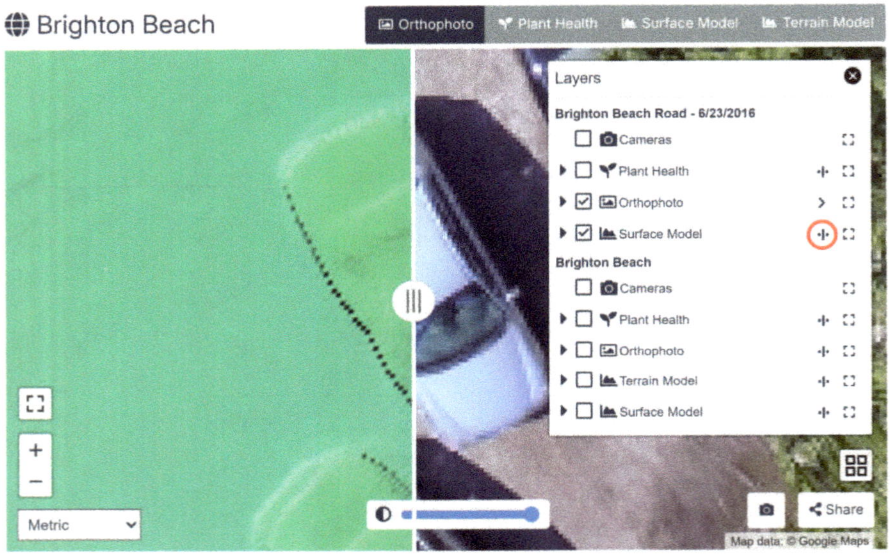

You can compare layers from the same task or from different tasks

Crop Results

WebODM supports interactive, non-destructive cropping. From the **Map** view you can click the **Crop** button to define a crop area, which will affect maps, elevation models and point clouds. Cropping is always reversible, e.g. if you decide you want to remove or re-define the crop area, you can simply press the crop button a second time. You can also hold the *shift* key on the keyboard while drawing the crop area to enforce straight lines.

Cropping is a safe operation, you can always revert it

The crop operation also affects the 3D outputs. When you open the **3D** view, the crop bounds will apply to the point cloud and textured model display. Note however than the textured 3D model will not be cropped if you download it.

Make Measurements

Both **Map** and **3D** view have measurement tools. From **Map** view, click the **Measure volume, area and length** button from the right side. From **3D** view, under the **Tools** menu you'll find several measurement tools.

Measurements made in the 3D view are persistent, which means they will be saved and restored if you reload the page. Those made in the Map view currently are *not* persistent, but you can export them to GeoJSON and re-import them by dragging and dropping the GeoJSON file back into the map.

Generate Contours

If a task was processed with a DSM or a DTM, from **Map** view you can open the **Contours** panel to generate contour lines from the elevation models.

Add Media Files

You can associate a task with additional media files such as videos, 360° equirectangular panoramas and images. These can sometimes be useful to add additional documentation to a map.

To add media files, from the **Dashboard** find the **...** button to the right of a task and click **Media**

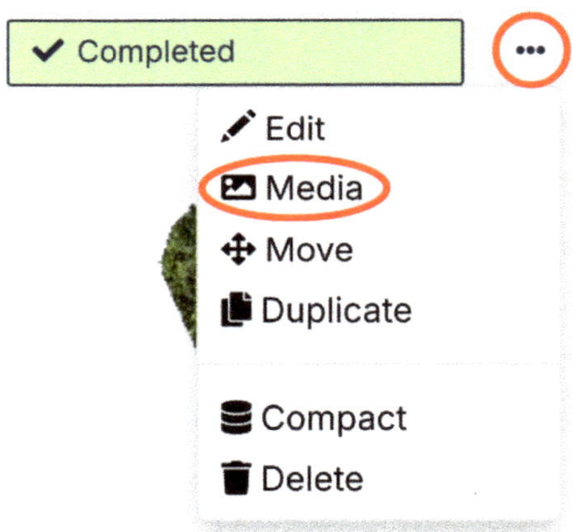

After uploading media files, you can optionally add descriptions to each file by switching to **List View** and pressing the **+** button.

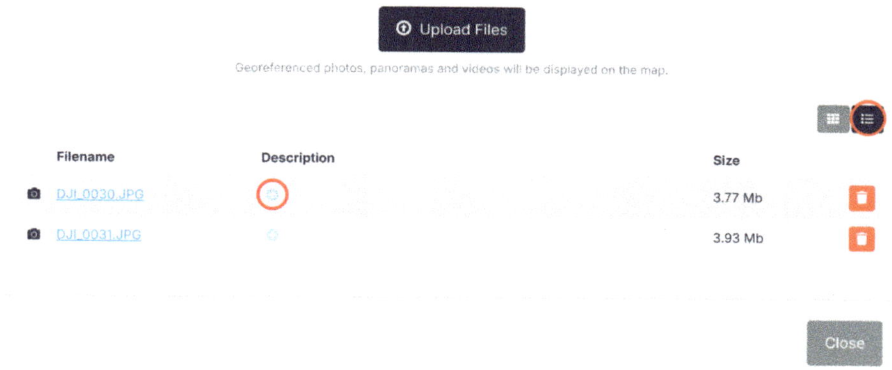

Media management panel

All media files that have georeferencing will be available from the **Map** view. To display them, open the **Layers** panel and toggle the **Media** layer.

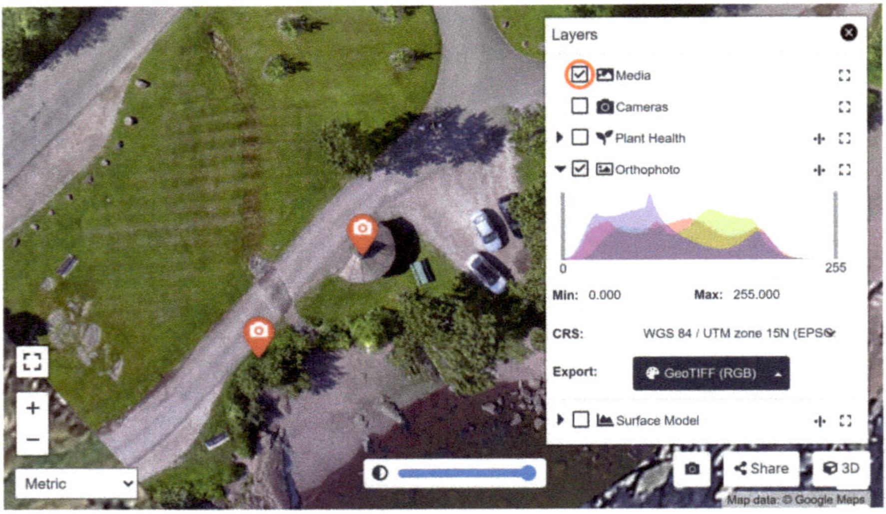

Clicking on a marker will display the media file. Each media type is displayed differently

Media Type	Displays
Panorama	A 360° interactive viewer
Video	A video + flight path display
Image	A fullscreen image display

After uploading video files, the program will automatically attempt to extract the georeferencing data. If georeferencing data is stored in a separate .SRT file, you can upload it alongside the video, making sure the .SRT filename matches the video. For example, upload both **my-video.mp4** and **my-video.srt**.

Import External Assets

It's possible to import maps, elevation models and point clouds that have been processed outside of WebODM, for example from other photogrammetry software. To do that, from the **Dashboard** click **Import — External Data**. Data imported this way is stored as a new task inside of a project.

Export Tasks To Another WebODM

Tasks can also be downloaded and imported between WebODM installations. To do that, download a task's backup by pressing **Download — Backup** and subsequently pressing the **Import — Assets / Backups** button from the **Dashboard**.

The difference between **All Assets** and **Backup** is that a backup includes all assets, plus the original images used for processing as well as the task's metadata such as title, tags, processing options and any 3D measurements made from the 3D view.

Manage Plugins

Some functionality in WebODM is implemented via plugins. By default many plugins are enabled and some are disabled. They can be toggled on/off by visiting **Administration — Plugins**.

Change The Look and Feel

You can customize the colors, logos and names of WebODM by visiting the **Administration — Theme** and **Administration — Brand** panels.

Customize the Basemaps

The list of basemaps that is available from **Map** view can be changed by visiting the **Administration — Basemaps** panel.

Create New Users & Groups

You can create user accounts (and groups) for people in your organization by visiting the **Administration — Accounts** panel.

Each user and group can be assigned different permissions, such as whether a user is able to create new projects, use certain processing nodes and so forth.

User permissions are set by navigating to **Administration — Accounts** or **Administration — Groups** and selecting an entry.

By default new users are assigned to a **Default** group and inherit some basic permissions, such as the ability to create and manage projects, presets and tasks.

Note that permissions in WebODM can be set with fine granularity to individual projects and processing nodes. For example, a user having the **nodeodm | Processing Node | Can view Processing Node** permission does not automatically give that user access to use all processing nodes. If you create and log-in with a new user that doesn't have the status of Administrator (also called **superuser**), you will notice that the **node-odx-1** node doesn't appear in the list of available processing nodes. To make the processing node available to the new user, you need to log-in with your administrator account and navigate to **Processing Nodes — node-odx-1 — Edit — Object Permissions**.

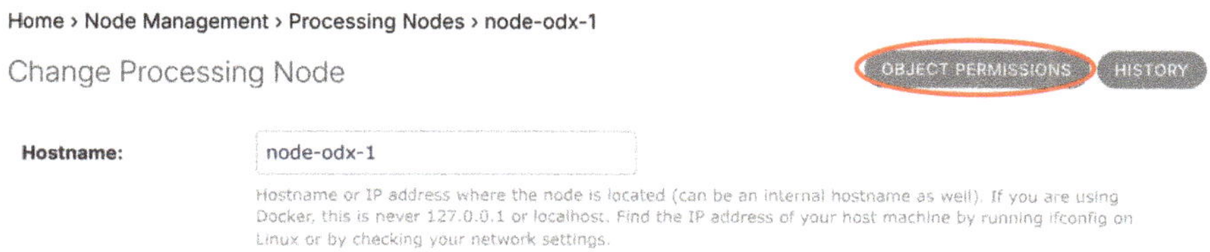

Then under **Users**, type the name of the user you want to allow to access the processing node, click the **Manage user** and assign the **Can view Processing Node** permission. **Save** the changes and the user will now be able to use the processing node.

Project Permissions

By default a project is owned by the user that created it. All tasks that are part of a project inherit the permissions from that project. Administrator users have access to everything, while normal users have only access to the tasks they have created. To share a project between users press the **Edit** link from a project:

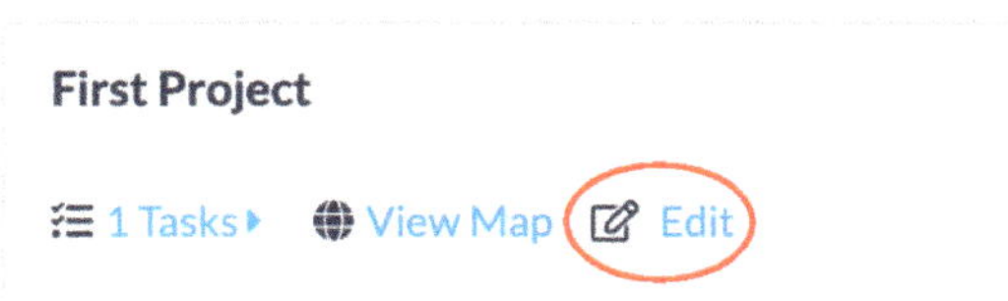

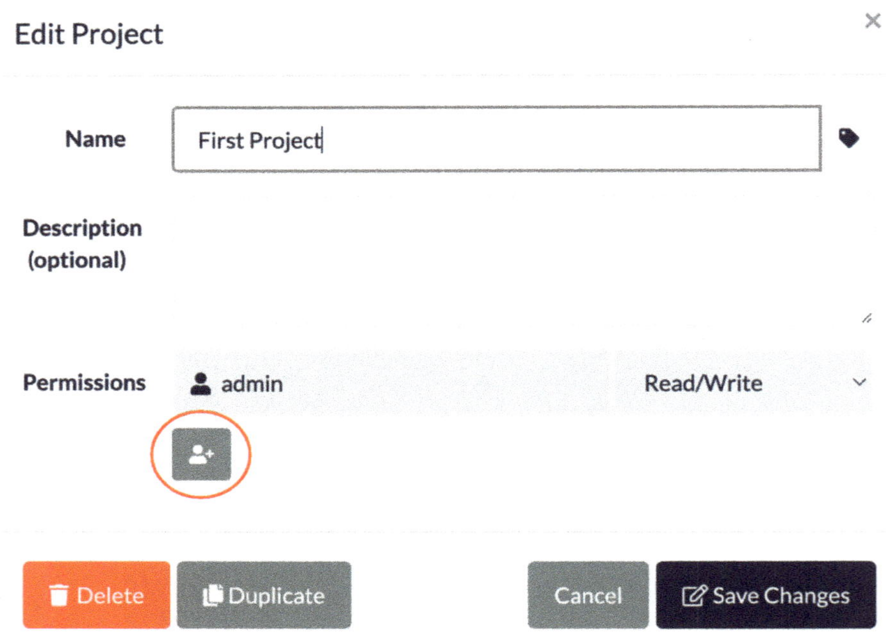

Project permissions dialog

Clicking the button next to **Permissions** will allow you to give access to more users or groups, either with **Read** or **Read/Write** access.

Managing Tags

Projects and tasks can be assigned one or more optional **tags**. This is a convenient way to organize projects and tasks with user-defined labels. Tags can be assigned by clicking the icon next to a project or task name. The tags can also be rearranged by clicking and dragging them.

Tags are great for organizing projects and tasks

5. The Processing Pipeline

> "Any sufficiently advanced technology is indistinguishable from magic." - *Arthur C. Clarke*

If this was the first time you've used a software like WebODM, or if you can remember the first time you used it, it's likely that at some point you had a ***woah!*** moment: how could a computer take simple 2D images and turn them into georeferenced mosaics, 3D models and point clouds?

Going from images to 3D models and orthophotos is a process best visualized as a series of incremental steps. Each step relies on the work of previous steps.

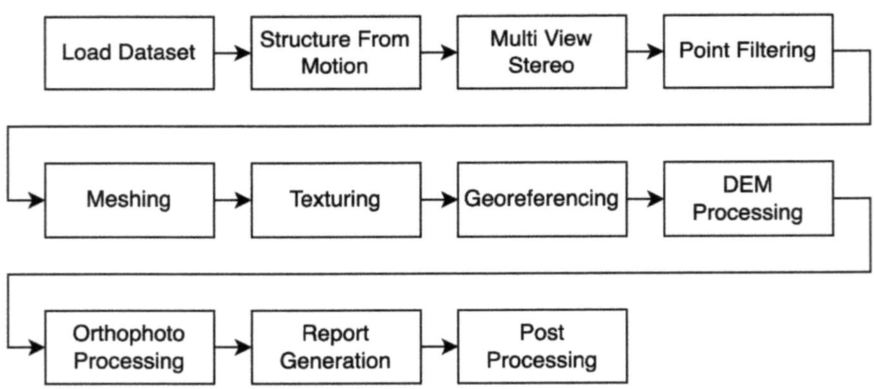

WebODM's processing pipeline

In this chapter we will explore an overview of the pipeline. We will not cover too many details, as each step's behavior can be tweaked by changing the task options. We will discuss in depth of how task options affect the inner workings of the pipeline in the next chapter.

Load Dataset

This step extracts GPS and orientation information from the EXIF tags of good (non corrupted) images. GCP and GEO files, as well as image masks (covered in another chapter) are also validated. This step is also responsible for automatically generating image masks when certain task options are used. If GPS information or GCPs are available, a geographical center point is determined. This point (offset) is used as an anchor to allow conversion from local to geographical coordinates in later steps. If video files are detected, still image frames from the videos are extracted.

Input: images/videos + GCP (optional) + GEO (optional) + image masks (optional)

Output: image database, image masks, video frames, georeferencing offset

Structure From Motion

Structure From Motion (SFM) is a photogrammetry technique for estimating 3D objects (structures) from overlapping image sequences (from the motion of a camera taking pictures). At a very high level, the idea of SFM begins from the intuition that we can perceive a whole lot of information about a scene by just observing it from multiple view points. Using perspective geometry and optics, the position and orientation of the camera can be recovered for every picture. Astute readers might wonder why this is needed. After all, doesn't every picture already embed GPS and gimbal information? One of the problems is that GPS information (without Real Time Kinematics, a technique used to improve GPS accuracy) is not all that precise and gimbal information is not always present. SFM is much more accurate in calculating the position of cameras. As a bonus, it doesn't require any GPS information at all.

SFM performs several sequential steps:

- Loads the camera information from the image database. The optics equations require a good estimate of the camera parameters (focal length, sensor size and others) for the process to work. The information from the image database is used as a best guess initial estimate which is refined in later steps.
- Each image is scanned for easily identifiable points of interest, such as edges and corners of objects. These points of interest are also called features. This is a critically important step. Take a look at the image below:

Two pictures of a white wall (top) vs. two pictures of a shark (bottom). Can you tell the camera moved left?

If we take two pictures of a white wall, we cannot tell how they relate to each other (did we move the camera left or right?). Compare them with the two pictures of the shark.

In the second set of pictures we can tell that our camera has moved left (and tilted a bit). A computer cannot recognize any movement in the white wall pictures, which makes it impossible to solve the SFM problem. Next time you wonder why that grass field shot at low altitude does not want to be reconstructed, you'll know why: likely not enough identifiable features!

- Image features from the previous step are now compared with each other. When many features are shared between two images (the same objects appear in two pictures) the images are matched. Some optimizations are employed to remove likely impossible candidates, such as images that are far away from each other using GPS information.

- Starting from a single pair of images and progressively adding more images, the program begins to recover the positions and orientations of the cameras as well as generating a *sparse* collection of triangulated points (a sparse point cloud). This is accomplished using knowledge of optics (the physics laws that govern light and in this case its interaction with camera lenses), perspective geometry (the studies about representing 3D objects on 2D surfaces) and approximation methods for generating a consistent estimate of the camera information, orientation and position of the resulting triangulated points.

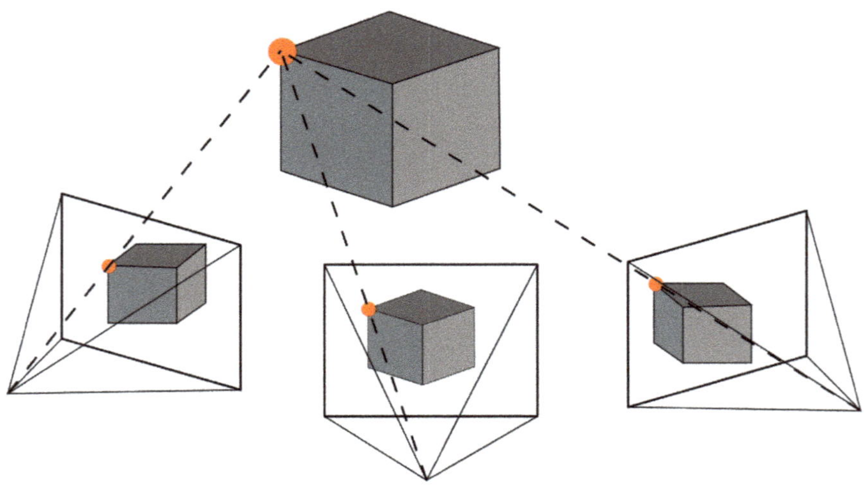

The SFM problem. What kind of camera took these pictures and where was the camera when the pictures were taken?

Photogrammetry is not a new field and its history dates back hundreds of years[1]. It's just that we've recently discovered that computers can be really good at it. For those interested in learning more about SFM, Cyrill Stachniss from the University of Bonn published some really good lectures on YouTube[2]. ODX uses a software package called OpenSfM[3] (Open Structure From Motion) for efficiently solving the SFM problem.

Input: images + image database + GCP (optional)

Output: camera poses + sparse point cloud + statistics

Multi View Stereo

While SFM focuses mostly on the estimation of camera poses, Multi-View Stereo (MVS) focuses on the reconstruction of 3D models from multiple overlapping image pairs. MVS programs expect that information about cameras has already been computed and this allows them to focus on one thing: create a highly detailed set of 3D points (a *dense point cloud*). WebODM's internal photogrammetry engine, ODX, uses a software called OpenMVS[4] to efficiently solve the MVS problem.

[1] History of Photogrammetry: masseranolabs.com/History_of_photogrammetry.pdf

[2] Online Course: Photogrammetric Computer Vision Block: youtube.com/playlist?list=PLgnQpQtFTOGTPQhKBOGgjTgX-mzpsOGOX

[3] OpenSfM: github.com/OpenSfM/OpenSfM

[4] OpenMVS: github.com/cdcseacave/openMVS

Lots of 3D points make a dense point cloud

Input: images + camera poses + sparse point cloud

Output: dense point cloud

Point Filtering

Errors during the SFM/MVS steps can sometimes generate some amount of stray points, also referred to as outliers. ODX reduces the amount of outliers by filtering the dense point cloud using statistical methods.

Input: dense or sparse point cloud

Output: filtered point cloud

Meshing

When you think of a *3D model* you most likely imagine the type of models you see in videogames or movies. These models are more precisely called *polygonal meshes* or *meshes* for short.

3D mesh

Whenever a 3D model is scanned or derived from a photogrammetry process, the result is typically represented with 3D points. To go from 3D points to polygonal meshes we have to perform two steps:

1. "Connect the dots" using many triangles to obtain a mesh. Points may be moved or eliminated to create a better looking mesh.
2. Add color to the mesh (a process referred to as *texturing*).

Meshing is the process of "connecting the dots". ODX supports two different algorithms for meshing and uses one or the other depending on the situation and the user settings:

1. Screened Poisson Surface Reconstruction is a robust, memory efficient and battle tested algorithm for creating 3D surfaces by Michael Kazhdan[5]. It's used for generating full 3D models with a high degree of accuracy.
2. dem2mesh[6] is a program I developed for generating 2.5D meshes. 2.5D

[5]Screened Poisson Surface Reconstruction: cs.jhu.edu/~misha/Code/PoissonRecon
[6]dem2mesh: github.com/WebODM/dem2mesh

meshes are meshes that look 3D, but are simple *extrusions* of a 2D surface. These are used for generating orthophotos, as orthophotos do not require full 3D models for rendering and results often tend to look better.

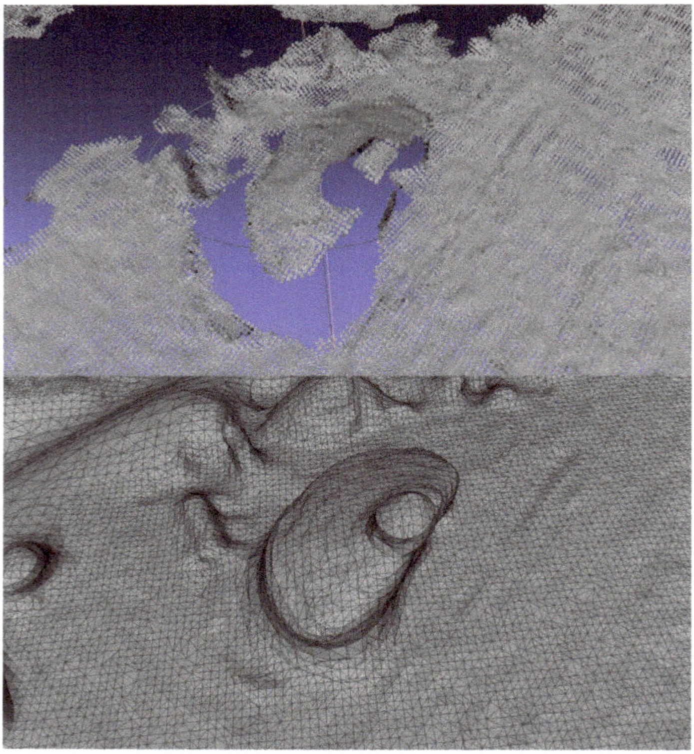

From 3D points to mesh

Input: filtered point cloud

Output: 3D and 2.5D meshes

Texturing

At this point the mesh does not have any colors. It's just a polygon soup. Texturing is the process of adding colors to meshes. It does so by using specially computed images (texture images) and by assigning each polygon to a section of the texture images. The process of creating the texture images and creating the associated mappings is performed by MvsTexturing[7], a software initially developed at TU Darmstadt that has been modified for ODX. At a very high level the program works as follows:

- Loads camera poses and images from the SFM process.
- Loads the mesh.
- For each polygon in the mesh, it finds the best image to fill it.
- It creates one or more texture images based on the information from the step above, also checking and attempting to remove moving objects (cats, cars, etc.).
- Sections of the texture images are color adjusted to compensate for differences in illumination.
- The borders (*seams*) between neighboring sections are blended to reduce color differences.

[7]MvsTexturing: github.com/nmoehrle/mvs-texturing

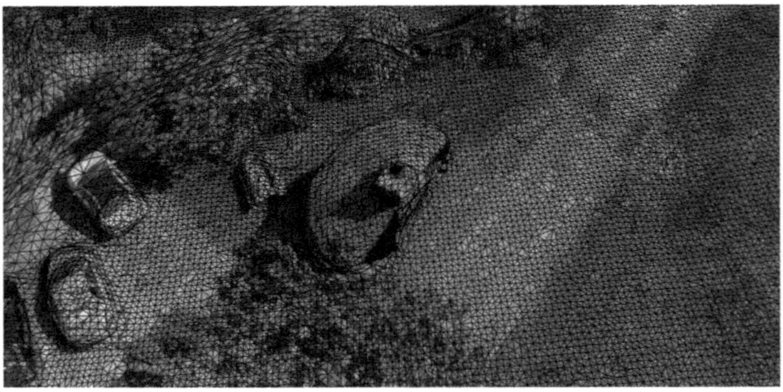

Textured mesh

Due to some randomness in the texturing algorithm, you are not guaranteed to get the same results if you run the process twice on the same mesh. That's why you might notice that the same dataset processed twice yields slightly different looking models (and orthophotos).

Input: images + camera poses + meshes

Output: textured meshes

Georeferencing

Up to this point all outputs have been represented using a *local* coordinate system. Coordinates in this system don't directly represent locations on earth. Georeferencing is the process of converting (*transforming*) a local coordinate system into a world coordinate system. ODX can do this only if location information about the world is available, either via GPS information or GCPs. When GPS information is available, it is incorporated during the SFM step to align the reconstruction as to minimize the error between the GPS information and the computed camera positions. When GCPs are available, the GPS information is ignored and GCPs are used for the alignment instead.

During this step it's also possible to perform the alignment with another elevation source, such as the point cloud of the same area from another reconstruction. We discuss this workflow more in detail in the next chapter.

Once georeferenced, the point cloud is used to generate an estimate of the geographical boundaries of the dataset. These boundaries are used in subsequent steps for cropping orthophotos and digital elevation models (DEMs).

Input: georeferencing offset + point cloud + alignment file (optional)

Output: georeferenced point cloud + crop boundaries

Digital Elevation Model Processing

Point clouds are cool to look at, but much analysis is usually done using simpler 2D DEMs, which represent XY coordinates as pixel locations on the screen and pixel intensities (or colors) as elevation values. During this step ODX takes the georeferenced point cloud and extracts a surface model by using gridding methods. If there are any holes in the model (perhaps an area is missing), they are filled using interpolation. Finally, the model is smoothed using a median filter to remove noise (bad values). With certain settings it can also classify the point cloud and generate a terrain model by first removing all non-ground points. Finally, the results are cropped.

Digital surface model

Input: georeferenced point cloud + crop boundaries

Output: digital surface models + digital terrain models + classified georeferenced point cloud

Orthophoto Processing

The orthophoto is generated by taking a picture of the textured 3D mesh from the top. A dedicated program loads the textured mesh into an orthographic scene and saves the result to an image using the appropriate resolution. The image is then georeferenced and converted to a GeoTIFF using the information computed in the georeferencing step. Finally, the result is cropped.

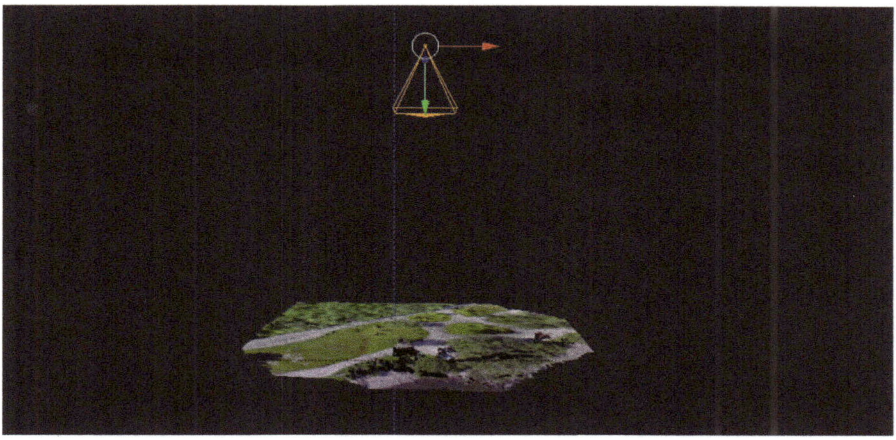

Orthographic camera taking a picture of the 3D model from the top

Orthophoto

Input: textured mesh + crop boundaries

Output: orthophoto

Report Generation

A PDF report along with other data is generated at this step.

Input: statistics

Output: PDF report

Post Processing

ODX has the ability to generate OGC 3D Tiles[8] point clouds and 3D models at this step and perform other post processing tasks.

Input: georeferenced point cloud + textured mesh

Output: OGC 3D Tiles (optional)

We covered a general overview of the processing pipeline. We avoided going into too much detail about the specific implementation of each step, since any effort to discuss implementation details would inevitably become inaccurate or obsolete very quickly. The beauty of open source is that you don't need a manual to tell you the details of the implementation. Those interested can and are encouraged to go look for details directly from the source code[9].

Now we turn our eyes to one of the most practical and important topics of this book: mastering the long list of task options and understanding what in the world each one does.

[8] OGC 3D Tiles: ogc.org/standard/3dtiles/

[9] ODX Stages Source Code: github.com/WebODM/ODX/tree/master/stages

6. Task Options in Depth

There are several steps involved in the data processing pipeline. Each step has several adjustable settings that influence the output. The software exposes a subset of these available knobs through various options. When creating a task, a user can choose to tweak one or more options to change the behavior of the pipeline.

Options by default are displayed by category, but they can also be displayed alphabetically. To do that, click the list view button from the top right side of the dialog.

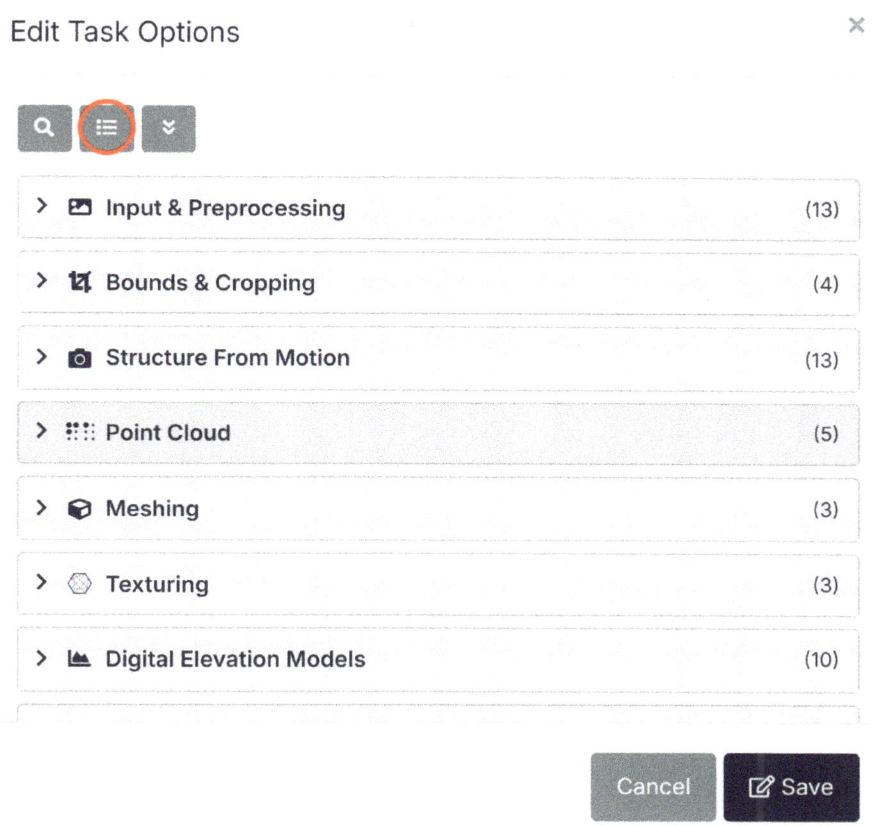

Options as shown in WebODM when creating a task

Tuning options is more art than science. That's mostly because the best options for certain datasets do not automatically transfer to others. As a general rule, one should start with the defaults, which work fairly well for most datasets and apply tweaks as needed.

A quick note about large language models (LLMs) is warranted here. Many people are turning to these tools for help in picking good processing settings. I must warn that as of 2026 LLMs are *pretty bad* at giving advice when it comes to tuning WebODM options, while sounding very confident in doing so[1].

This chapter is about understanding in detail what each option does. By the end of the chapter you'll be able to quickly improve your results, explain why certain models turn out the way they do and know what to tweak if the results don't turn out the way you want.

A few of these options might be hidden in WebODM and available only from ODX. This is because sometimes the option does not make sense in the context of the graphic interface workflow, or it's simply not supported.

When there is some math to explain, I write the formulas using Python because it's easier than math notation and can be typed on a computer. You can copy/paste the code on a website such as online-python.com and follow along even if you don't know Python.

Feel free to jump around and use this chapter as a reference. As the software gets better, some of these options might disappear from future versions and new ones might be introduced. The list below is taken from the software as of April 28th 2026. In alphabetical order:

3d-tiles

OGC 3D Tiles[2] are a format specification for visualization and interaction with 3D geospatial content. These files can be displayed with software such as the open source virtual globe engine Cesium[3]. ODX has support for generating point clouds and textured 3D models in 3D Tiles format by turning on this option (and doesn't rely on third party services to do so).

[1]The bs machines: thebullshitmachines.com
[2]OGC 3D Tiles: ogc.org/standard/3dtiles/
[3]Cesium: github.com/CesiumGS/cesium

align

This option can be useful when processing datasets of the same area, perhaps captured at different times. It instructs ODX to discard the alignment information from GPS or GCPs and to use a georeferenced point cloud or DEM GeoTIFF as a reference to align the reconstruction to.

In WebODM this option is not shown in the options list, because it's made available via a convenient user interface. To use it, create a second task to be aligned to an existing task in the same project as the first. Then use the **Alignment** field to select the task you want to align your new task to. Make sure the tasks are in the same project and that they overlap with each other, otherwise the alignment field will not be displayed.

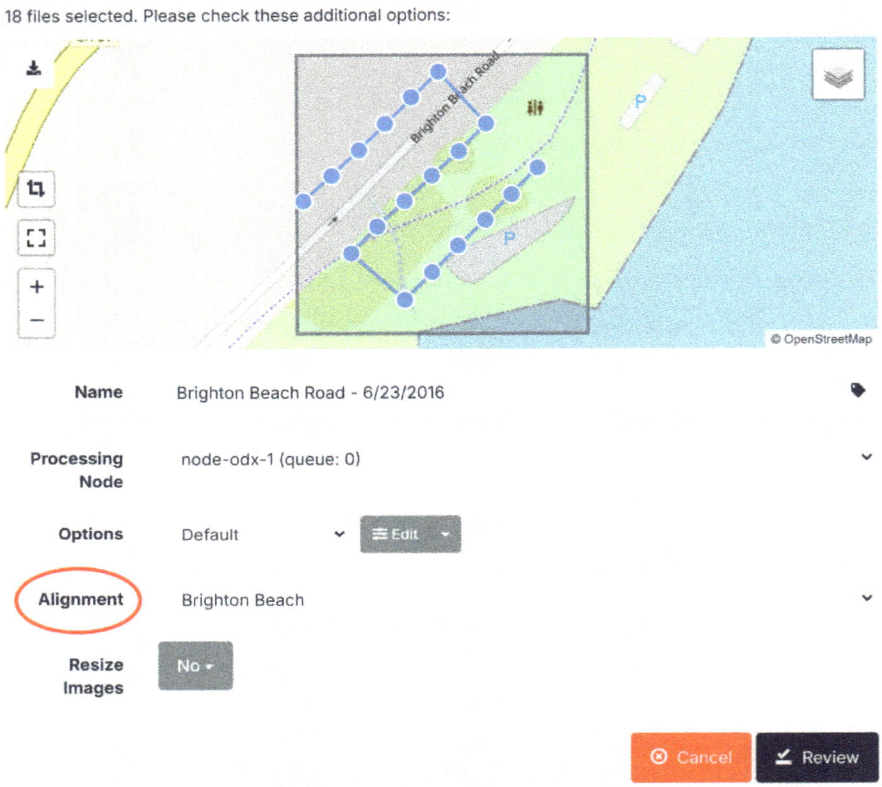

Alignment selection

There's currently no way to change the alignment file and restart a task. You will need to create a new task and reprocess from the beginning.

With ODX (command line) the workflow is usually the following:

- Process dataset #1.
- Download the point cloud of dataset #1.
- Process dataset #2, but use the `align` option with the point cloud of #1.

- Dataset #2 is now aligned to #1.

ODX performs the alignment using CODEM[4], a state-of-the-art method for 3D model alignment. Internally, CODEM performs alignment via a two step process:

1. A rough (coarse) alignment is performed by converting the point cloud to an elevation image (raster), extracting point of interest and matching them between the source and target elevation models. This is similar to how SFM matches images.
2. A finer alignment is performed by comparing the location of 3D points between the models (using an iterative closest point algorithm, or ICP[5]).

[4]CODEM: github.com/NCALM-UH/CODEM
[5]Iterative Closest Point: en.wikipedia.org/wiki/Iterative_closest_point

Alignment Errors Details

	DSM (Coarse)	ICP (Fine)	RMS Error
X Error (meters)	1.120	0.261	1.381
Y Error (meters)	2.252	0.249	2.502
Z Error (meters)	0.386	0.231	0.617
3D Error (meters)	2.545	0.429	2.974

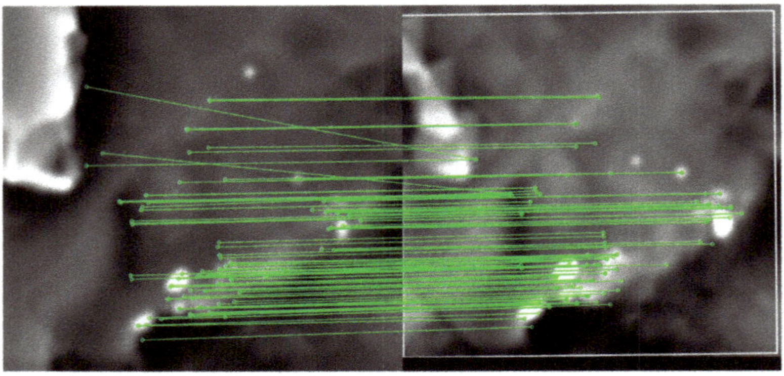

On successful alignment the PDF report will display the alignment results

Root Mean Square (RMS) is probably the most interesting metric. It's an estimate of the average error you can expect from the alignment.

3D Error is the error across X/Y/Z dimensions, computed using the Pythagorean theorem:

```
import math
x, y, z = (1.120, 2.252, 0.386)
error = math.sqrt(x**2 + y**2 + z**2)
print(error) # <-- ~2.545
```

auto-boundary

Automatically computes a 2D polygon surrounding the locations of all camera poses (as computed during SFM), then uses that polygon as an argument for the boundary option. The polygon is computed using a *convex hull* and by adding a *distance buffer* proportional to the flight altitude, where higher altitude = larger distance.

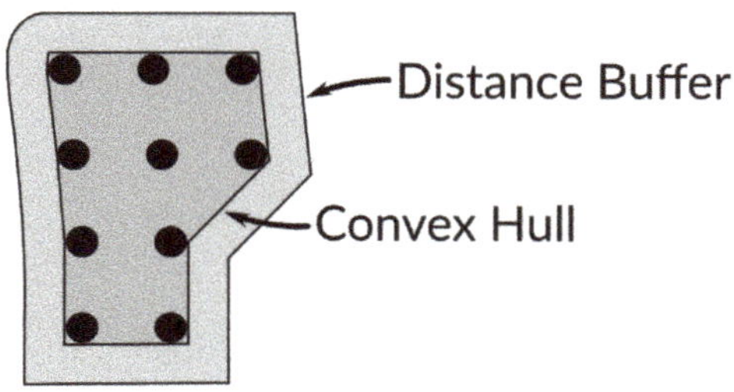

Boundary computed from camera poses (dots)

See boundary for more information.

auto-boundary-distance

Manually override the *distance buffer* value (in meters) of auto-boundary.

bg-removal

Uses artificial intelligence methods to automatically generate image masks that remove the background. This is useful for creating 3D models of individual objects:

Image of a banana (left) and background mask computed from the image (right)

3D model without masking (left) and with background masking (right)

This option can be useful to get a clean reconstruction of a target object. For aerial scenes this option is not very useful. See the sky-removal option instead.

See also the image masks chapter.

boundary

This option allows a user to specify a single polygon boundary (in GeoJSON[6] format) which is used to filter the point cloud. Any point that falls *outside* the polygon is discarded. This is often useful for removing outlier points that might appear as a result of capturing oblique shots, or for limiting the area of a reconstruction. Note that since this type of filtering is done on the point cloud, it also affects every other output (3D models, orthophotos and DEMs).

You can create GeoJSON polygons using a program such as QGIS[7] or online at geojson.io. It can also be automatically generated via the auto-boundary option.

The boundary polygon can also be used as the crop area for DEMs and orthophotos if the crop option is set to zero.

In WebODM after selecting some input images, from the map preview panel it's possible to draw a polygon that automatically sets this option and crop to zero:

[6] GeoJSON: en.wikipedia.org/wiki/GeoJSON
[7] QGIS: qgis.org

Drawing a boundary from map preview

When used from the command line, this option can point to a path to a GeoJSON file.

build-overviews

When set, overviews are added to the orthophoto. This does not affect DEMs. Overviews are an optimization available for GeoTIFFs that reduces the time it takes to open them, for the tradeoff of a larger filesize and some computational time. Think of overviews as downsized copies of the orthophoto, stored inside the orthophoto file itself. Overviews are useful when opening the orthophoto in GIS programs that support them, such as QGIS. When overviews are available, the viewer program can load the overview most appropriate for the current zoom level instead of loading the entire file. If it takes forever to display a 400MB orthophoto in a GIS program, it's probably because overviews weren't built! ODX creates overviews at 1/2, 1/4, 1/8 and 1/16 of the original resolution using an average interpolation. If an orthophoto is 1000x1000 pixels, **build-overviews** will store copies of the same orthophoto at 500, 250,

125 and 62 pixels resolution for faster visualization.

Note that this option is ignored if the cog option is also set, which is always the case for datasets processed with WebODM, since Cloud Optimized GeoTIFFs (COGs) have their own overviews. For this reason, this option is hidden in WebODM, but available from the command line.

camera-lens

Digital photos are created by reading values from a sensor. The sensor measures the amount of light that hits it. Before light hits the sensor, it passes through a lens. Camera lenses add various amount of distortion to photos and the lens shape determines the type of distortion. Some distortion is quite extreme as in the case of fisheye or wide-angle lenses, or subtle as in the case of perspective lenses. Note that some degree of distortion is always present.

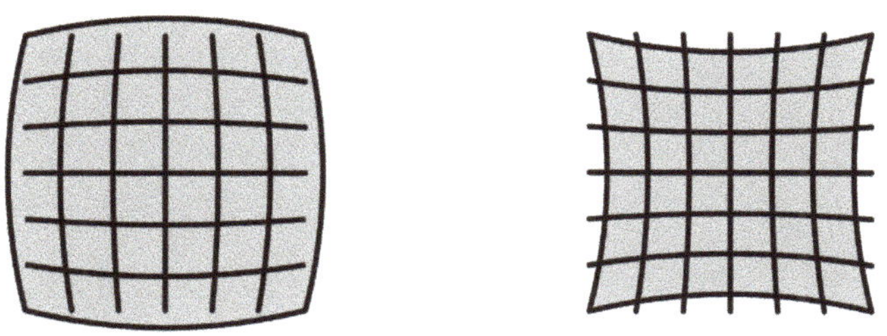

Examples of radial distortion: barrel (left) and pincushion (right)

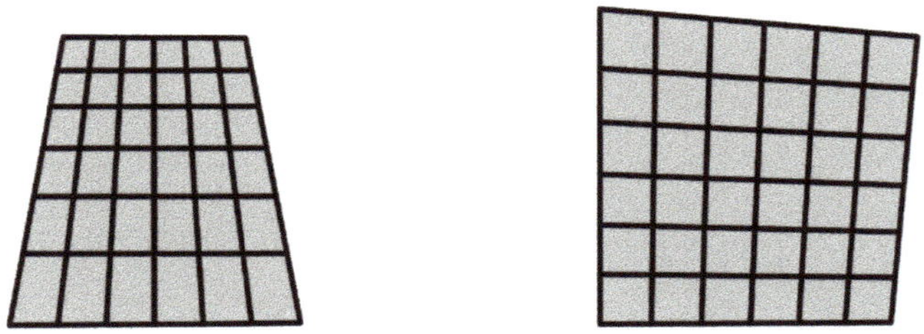

Misalignment between the lens and sensor can cause tangential distortions like these

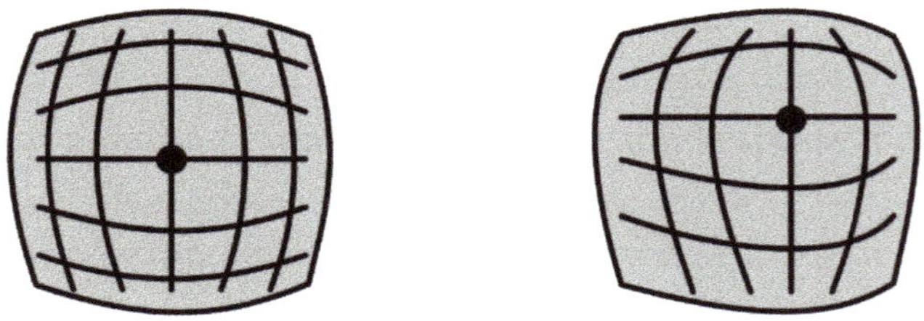

The principal point represents the center of the camera lens (left), but is often offset and affects the distortion model (exaggerated, right)

Over the years mathematical models have been formulated to represent and compensate for these distortions. ODX supports various models and chooses the best model based on the information that is available from the EXIF[8] and XMP[9] tags of the images. Often times, however, there's no such information. If you attempt to process images captured with a fisheye lens, but processing fails or the final results look like they came out of some strange universe, it's

[8] EXIF Tags: exiftool.org/TagNames/EXIF.html
[9] XMP Tags: exiftool.org/TagNames/XMP.html

likely that you need to manually specify `fisheye` or `fisheye_opencv` as the `camera-lens` option. As a general rule, if the input images have any significant distortion, it's always safest to manually set this option to the appropriate value.

Value	Images	Description
auto	Normal	Defaults to **brown**, unless the XMP tag `GPano:ProjectionType` or `Camera:ModelType` contains a value from this table
perspective	Normal	Handles radial distortion
brown	Normal	Handles radial, tangential and principal point distortions
fisheye	Ultra wide-angle	Handles radial distortion
fisheye_opencv	Ultra wide-angle	Handles radial distortion, tangential and principal point distortions
spherical	360	Handles spherical projection for 360 images
equirectangular	360	Same as *spherical* (legacy name)
dual	Ultra wide-angle / Normal	Handles radial distortion from sensors that can capture both fisheye and perspective images, transitioning from one to the other.

Note that using this option sets the same camera lens model for all images, even if they are from different cameras. To use different cameras with different models, images need to have the proper XMP tags set.

cameras

By default, during SFM, the camera model's distortion parameters are estimated from the input images. By using this option it's possible to choose a precomputed set of parameters instead, either as a path to a **cameras.json** file or by providing the contents of a **cameras.json** file. A **cameras.json** file is always computed after processing a dataset, so you can use the camera parameters computed from one dataset to process another. Specifying a precomputed set of camera parameters can be useful to increase the accuracy of certain reconstructions, especially those that exhibit *doming* effects (point clouds that look concave or convex when they should be straight). We cover usage of this option in more detail in the Camera Calibration chapter.

cog

A Cloud Optimized GeoTIFF (COG) is a regular GeoTIFF file, but optimized for being hosted and streamed over the internet[10]. This option is not displayed in WebODM because by default it is always turned on. With ODX you need to manually turn it on. By turning on this option, orthophotos and DEMs will be generated as Cloud Optimized GeoTIFFs.

[10] Cloud Optimized GeoTIFF: cogeo.org

copy-to

With this option you can specify a path to a folder where to copy all processed output results. This can be useful for some command line automation scripts workflows. This option is hidden in WebODM.

crop

In their raw form, orthophotos and DEMs contain irregular, jagged edges. These are the result of interpolation trying to fill areas that have little or no information. Cropping attempts to remove those edges to give us a nice, smooth looking output. The boundaries of the reconstruction are estimated by looking at the filtered point cloud. A polygon boundary is first computed and saved in *odm_georeferencing/odm_georeferenced_model.bounds.gpkg*. Then, this polygon is further smoothed and shrunk by the value specified in the **crop** option (in meters). The final polygon is then used to crop orthophotos and DEMs.

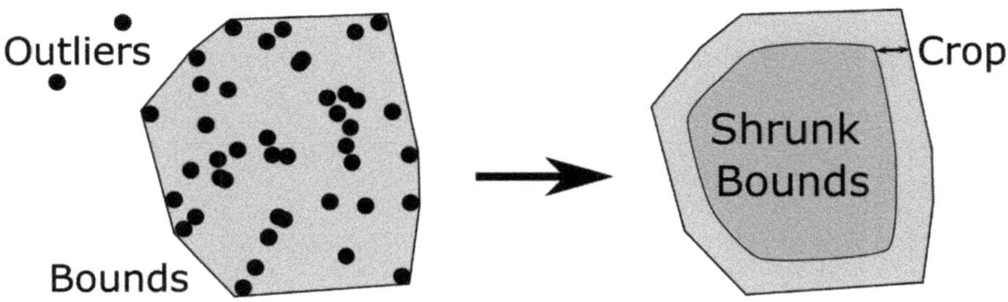

Point cloud (left) and shrunk bounds that define the crop area (right)

Estimating where the bounds are is not a perfect science. Sometimes the area of an orthophoto that looks perfectly good will be removed in the cropping process. This option can be set to zero to skip cropping. For very large datasets, skipping crop can lower the run-time, since no computations have to be performed to estimate the polygon boundary.

One can also set the boundary option and set this option to zero to manually define the crop area.

dem-decimation

All DEMs are computed from the point cloud. The larger the point cloud, the longer it takes to compute a DEM. To speed things up, at the trade-off of possible accuracy loss, this option reduces (decimates) the number of points used to compute DEMs. The value specifies how many points to "skip" during decimation. Let's look at an example by setting this option to 3. By taking all the points in the point cloud and placing them in a straight line, the program will reduce the number of points by keeping one every three.

Only black points are included. Gray points are skipped

This way ~33% of all points are included, and ~66% are removed. If you use a value of 1 (the default), then all points are included. If you use a value of 50, then ~2% of the original points are kept and ~98% are removed. You can compute this percentage by doing:

```
decimation = 50
print((1 / decimation) * 100) # <-- 2%
```

It should be noted that points are skipped sequentially and do not take into account spatial information, so this option should be used with care. Decimation also does not affect the original point cloud. The decimation is only used for the purpose of computing DEMs.

dem-euclidean-map

An euclidean map is a georeferenced image derived from DEMs (before any holes are filled) where each pixel represents the geometric distance of each pixel to the nearest *void, null* or *NODATA* pixel. It's an indicator (map) of how far a value in the DEM is to an area where there are no values. This can be useful in cases when a person wishes to know which areas of a DEM were derived from actual point cloud values and which ones were filled with interpolation. Looking at the euclidean map, every pixel that has a value of zero indicates that the corresponding location on the DEM was filled with interpolation (because the distance of a *NODATA* pixel to itself is zero).

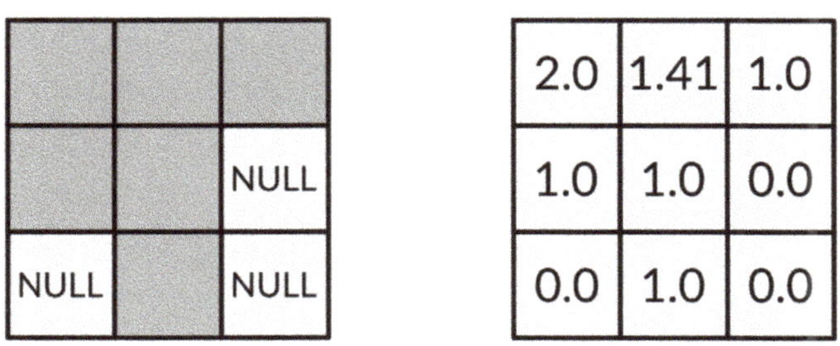

DEM before hole filling (left) and corresponding euclidean map (right)

Euclidean map results are stored in the *odm_dem* directory.

dem-gapfill-steps

The process of going from point cloud to DEMs is not as straightforward as it may seem. Since DEMs are *rasters* (images), they have *cells* (pixels). Each cell, should have a value. Depending on the resolution of the raster, certain cells may have zero, one or more points that fall into it. Every cell needs a value, even if no points fall directly into it, otherwise there will be empty areas (gaps) in the DEM! One way to overcome this is to use a radius around each cell. Every point that falls within the radius is considered part of the cell.

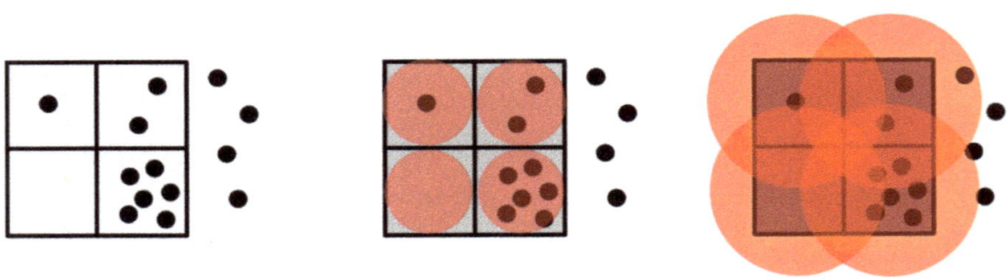

Pixels and points (left), radius of 0.5 (middle) and radius of 1 (right)

But how big should the radius be? If too small, as in the 0.5 radius example above, some cells might remain empty. If too big, there will be too much smoothing and accuracy will suffer. Since different point clouds have varying degrees of density, one solution is to compute multiple DEMs with different radiuses and stack them.

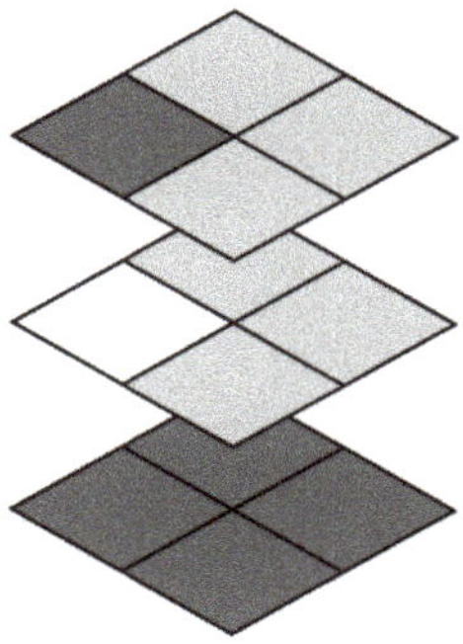

Gap fill interpolation with 2 DEM layers

Results with smaller radiuses (more accuracy, more gaps) are placed at the top, while results with bigger radiuses (less accuracy, less gaps) are placed at the bottom. If there are still gaps at the end of this process, any remaining gaps are filled using a less accurate smoothed nearest neighbor interpolation.

How many layers should there be? However many this option says there should be. The initial value for the radius for the first layer is set to an estimate of the average spacing between points in the point cloud. Subsequent layers have a radius that is the radius of their predecessors multiplied by the square root of two:

```
import math
radius = 0.2 # <-- average point cloud spacing
gapfill_steps = 3
for i in range(gapfill_steps):
    print(radius)
    radius = radius * math.sqrt(2)
# <-- 0.2 / 0.28 / 0.4
```

dem-resolution

This option specifies the output resolution of DEMs in cm / pixel.

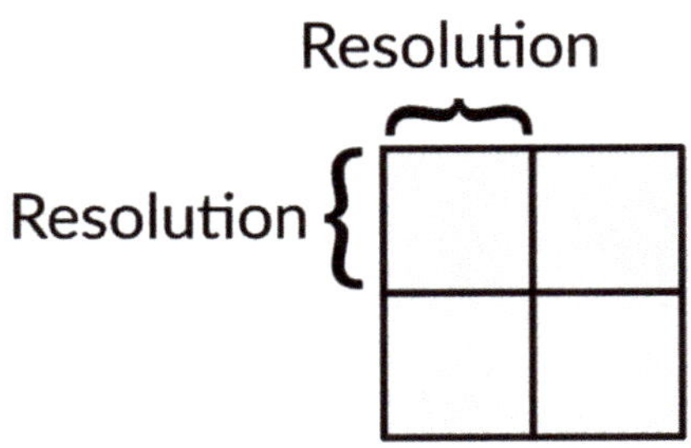

Each square represents a pixel in a raster DEM

As an example, if the area covered by the point cloud is 100x50 meters and dem-resolution is set to 10 cm / pixel, the final image size of the DEM in pixels can be calculated by:

```
width, height = (100, 50) # meters
dem_resolution = 10 # centimeters
cm_to_m = 100 # centimeters in one meter

print(width * cm_to_m / dem_resolution) # <-- 1000 pixels
print(height * cm_to_m / dem_resolution) # <-- 500 pixels
```

So the output DEM will be an image of 1000x500 pixels.

dsm

This option generates a digital surface model (DSM). DSMs are generated by taking the maximum elevation values in a point cloud, including both terrain and other structures such as buildings or trees. If two points fall on top of each other, only the tallest point is used. Gaps in the point cloud are filled using the process described in dem-gapfill-steps. The result is stored in *odm_dem/dsm.tif*.

dtm

This option generates a digital terrain model (DTM). DTMs are generated by classifying the point cloud using a hybrid simple morphological filter[11] (SMRF) + artificial intelligence method. Enabling this option implicitly turns on the pc-classify option. Non-ground points are discarded before computing the DTM. Gaps in the point cloud are filled using the process described in dem-gapfill-steps. For more information on tweaking the classification algorithm, see the pc-classify option. The result is stored in *odm_dem/dtm.tif*.

DSM (left) vs. DTM (right)

[11] SMRF: A Simple Morphological Filter for Ground Identification of LIDAR Data. github.com/thomaspingel/smrf

end-with

The processing pipeline is composed of several steps and processing is executed sequentially. Sometimes the results don't turn out as expected or a user might wish to compare the results of using different options. Since changing an option sometimes affects only a certain stage of the pipeline, there's no need to execute every single step all the way to the end. By using this option, the program will stop the execution at the chosen step. Possible values (in order of execution) are:

Option	Stage
dataset	Load Dataset
split	Split
merge	Merge
opensfm	Structure From Motion
openmvs	Multi View Stereo
odm_filterpoints	Point Filtering
odm_meshing	Meshing
mvs_texturing	Texturing
odm_georeferencing	Georeferencing
odm_dem	DEM
odm_orthophoto	Orthophoto
odm_report	Report
odm_postprocess	Postprocess

This option is often used in conjunction with rerun-from.

fast-orthophoto

Sometimes all that a user wants is an orthophoto, generated as fast as possible, using the least amount of resources. When **fast-orthophoto** is used, the program is instructed to skip the expensive MVS step. Recall that SFM computes a sparse point cloud, while MVS generates a refined, denser point cloud.

Sparse (top) vs. dense (bottom) point cloud outputs

Both point clouds can be used to generate a mesh. However, it's better to have more points, as meshes can be created with more details. In the dense point cloud screenshot above, the building on the right side of the scene is well defined, but it's poorly represented in the sparse point cloud. Buildings are especially difficult to model without a dense point cloud, so this option tends to yield poor results in urban areas. For flat areas such as farmlands, however, the results are quite good, since there are fewer buildings or structures to model. This option also tends to work well with images captured from a really high altitude or with images that have less than 50% overlap (such as many historical aerial images).

Normal (top) vs. fast-orthophoto (bottom)

Comparing the two images above, the building and tennis court on the top are much more defined than the bottom, but the flat grass areas between the two are almost identical. This option can make a big difference in processing times, especially for very large datasets.

feature-quality

The SFM process begins by extracting points of interest (features) from the input images. In order to speed up this process, extraction is performed on a resized copy of the input images, which is determined by a scaling factor.

Option	Factor
ultra	1 (no scaling)
high	1/2 (default)
medium	1/4
low	1/8
lowest	1/16

For example, setting this option to **medium** will extract features from images that are 1/4 of the size of their originals. The default value is usually good for most use cases. This option does not affect the size of the images for other parts of processing. Changing this option will not affect the resolution of the orthophoto. In some cases, and somewhat counter-intuitively, lowering this option can help reconstruct datasets that have significant blur or lack features, like forest areas.

feature-type

ODX exposes several algorithms for extracting image features during SFM. For most consistent and reliable results, it's recommended to leave the default value of **dspsift**, although in certain scenes and situations it might be beneficial to use others. See the table below.

Option	Description
dspsift[12]	General-purpose, typically performs 5-15% better than **sift**
sift[13]	General-purpose, works well in most cases
akaze[14]	General-purpose, can perform better on scenes with fewer objects of interest (e.g. forests, vegetation)
hahog[15]	General-purpose, similar to **sift**. It's the only one that works with matcher-type **bow**
orb[16]	Fast, but does not work well with images that have scale variations (images taken at varying altitudes)

force-gps

If a GCP file is used, by default all GPS information is ignored and the reconstruction is georeferenced using the information from the GCP file only.

[12]DSP-SIFT: Domain-Size Pooling in Local Descriptors. arxiv.org/abs/1412.8556

[13]SIFT: Scale Invariant Feature Transform. cs.ubc.ca/~lowe/papers/ijcv04.pdf

[14]AKAZE: Accelerated-KAZE. KAZE is a Japanese word that means *wind* (a tribute to Iijima, the father of scale space analysis). masseranolabs.com/akaze.pdf

[15]HAHOG: Hessian Affine (point detector) + Histogram of Oriented Gradients (descriptor). github.com/OpenSfM/OpenSfM/blob/master/opensfm/src/features/src/hahog.cc

[16]ORB: an efficient alternative to SIFT or SURF. masseranolabs.com/orb.pdf

The assumption here is that the GCP information is of higher accuracy than GPS. However, if the GPS information is also of high accuracy (perhaps it's been RTK[17] corrected), turning on this option will instruct the program to use both GCP and GPS data for georeferencing.

gcp

By default ODX looks for a file named **gcp_list.txt** in the project directory. If it exists, it's used as a ground control point file to increase the georeferencing accuracy of the results. With this option users can specify an alternate path for the GCP file. Ground control points and the GCP file format are explained in more detail in the Ground Control Points chapter.

This option is not shown in WebODM and is automatically set if a GCP file is uploaded with a dataset.

geo

By default ODX looks for a file named **geo.txt** in the project directory. If it exists, it's used as a geolocation file to set/overwrite the GPS information of images. This option allows users to specify an alternate path. We cover geolocation files and their format in the Geolocation Files chapter.

This option is not shown in WebODM and is automatically set if a GEO file is uploaded with a dataset.

[17] RTK: Real Time Kinematic is a technique used to increase the accuracy of GPS positions using a stationary base station that sends out correctional data to the drone.

gltf

This option generates a binary glTF[18] version of the textured mesh. glTF is a modern 3D file format optimized for portability and size. It is stored in *odm_texturing/odm_textured_model_geo.glb*. You can use a viewer such as gltf-viewer.donmccurdy.com to view binary glTF files.

Note that these .GLB files generated by ODX require viewers to support the *KHR_draco_mesh_compression* extension. Being a modern file format, not every 3D program supports it. At the time of writing, MeshLab[19] does not support it, but Blender[20] does.

This option is not shown in WebODM, as it is automatically turned on for every dataset.

gps-accuracy

GPS information is accurate up to a certain degree. For example, an average GPS-enabled smartphone in clear skies and no obstructions can find its location within a 5 meters radius. An estimate of the GPS accuracy value is used to apply constraints during the SFM process in order to improve the georeferencing accuracy of the reconstruction.

Often times accuracy information is available from the XMP tags of the images. ODX uses **twice** the number (to account for under-estimation) indicated in any of the following tags.

- **drone-dji:RtkStdLon**

[18] glTF: registry.khronos.org/glTF
[19] MeshLab: meshlab.net
[20] Blender: blender.org

- **drone-dji:RtkStdLat**
- **drone-dji:RtkStdHgt**
- **Camera:GPSXYAccuracy**
- **GPSXYAccuracy**
- **Camera:GPSZAccuracy**
- **GPSZAccuracy**

If multiple tags are available, the maximum value is used. If no tags are available, ODX uses a default value of **10 meters**.

Note that different images can have different accuracy values.

Setting this option (expressed as a radius, in meters) overrides the value for all images.

gps-z-offset

This option adjusts all images' GPS vertical values (Z) by a constant. It has no effect on GCPs. This can be useful in cases when elevation values reported by a drone are inaccurate, or if the survey area is small, to compute orthometric heights.

help

Shows all possible options and exits.

ignore-gsd

To achieve good processing speed, the program relies on optimizations. One of these optimizations uses the average Ground Sampling Distance (GSD) value from all images (plus some buffer) to achieve two goals:

1) Put a cap on the resolution of orthophotos and DEMs.
2) Compute a good target size for the images when texturing 3D models and performing MVS.

The reason for placing a cap on resolutions is simple. While the program allows output resolutions to be set via orthophoto-resolution and dem-resolution, it can be tedious to estimate what the maximum resolution can be. For example, if photos are captured at 400ft, it makes no sense to set the resolution to 0.1 cm / pixel. The photos don't contain enough details to achieve that target resolution. So the optimization automatically lowers the resolution to a more reasonable value.

Similarly, when the program knows that the orthophoto is going to have a target resolution of 5 cm / pixel, it's wasteful to use full resolution images to create the textures for the 3D models. The orthophoto will be downsized anyway, so the program resizes the images prior to texturing, speeding things up and lowering memory usage. This also applies to the MVS process.

There's a caveat with this approach: the GSD value is computed by averaging the GSD value of all images in the scene. In certain scenarios, such as when a double-cross flight pattern at different altitudes is used, the resolution could be possibly capped at a value less than ideal.

When the resolution or quality of the outputs is lower than expected, turning on **ignore-gsd** can improve results. The trade-off is longer run-time and potentially much higher memory usage.

matcher-neighbors

The SFM process involves matching image pairs, that is, finding images that share features between them (images showing the same objects or points of interest). The naive, brute force approach is to compare each image against each other image. This results in an exhaustive, but slow search. Finding all images pairs in a 100 images dataset would require a lot of comparisons. To be exact, it would require:

```
print(100 * (100 - 1)) # <-- 9900 comparisons
```

This number increases rapidly with larger datasets. To speed things up, the program uses an optimization. The core idea is that when processing datasets collected in a uniform pattern, most images will be paired with images that are within a short distance from each other. Since each image often contains GPS information, the program can calculate very quickly an approximate list of which images are adjacent to others, and discard images that are far away from each other. This is called preemptive matching.

By default ODX uses a graph connectivity method to perform preemptive matching. This method takes the GPS location of each image and connects them with edges using a Delaunay triangulation[21]. If two images are connected by an edge, they are considered a pair. To produce more pairs, the method randomly moves the position of the GPS locations to produce several such graphs (50 in total). All pairs from all graphs are then considered for further matching.

[21] Delaunay Triangulation: en.wikipedia.org/wiki/Delaunay_triangulation

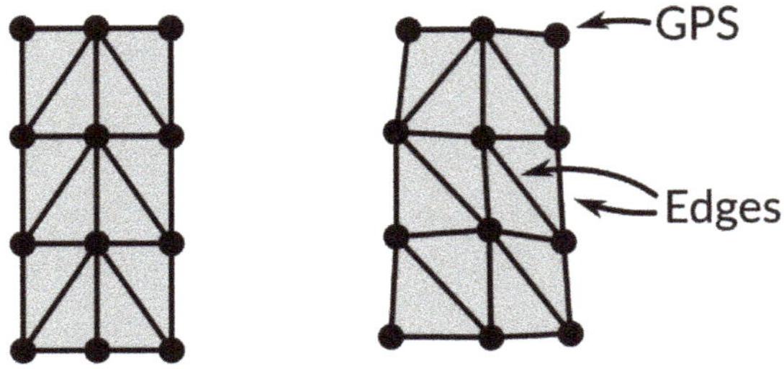

Initial graph (left) and graph with randomly moved positions and new edges (right). Every edge indicates an image pair

ODX also supports a different method to perform preemptive matching by considering only the nearest neighbors of each image instead of using a graph. It is enabled by setting this option. The illustration below shows the result of setting this option to 8:

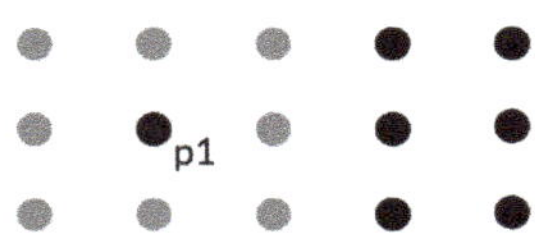

Dots represent approximate image locations, extracted from EXIF tags. When the matcher-neighbors is set to 8, only the 8 nearest neighbors (highlighted in gray) are considered for matching with image p1

This option can sometimes be beneficial for speeding up processing by reducing the number of matching pairs. If no GPS information is available, this option is disabled and all image pairs are considered, unless matcher-order is specified.

matcher-order

Similarly to matcher-neighbors, this option reduces the number of candidate pairs used for matching by using the sequential nature of image filenames. For example, if there are 3 images, which have been sorted by filename:

- **1.JPG**
- **2.JPG**
- **3.JPG**

And this option is set to 1, the program will consider matches between:

- **1.JPG** and **2.JPG**
- **2.JPG** and **3.JPG**

Because the "distance" between these image pairs from the list is 1. **1.JPG** and **3.JPG** have a distance of 2, so this pair will not be considered for matching.

The value of this option sets the maximum distance between image filenames for them to be considered a pair for matching. This option works only with datasets that lack GPS information. It's most useful for speeding up processing of images that are sequential, such as those extracted from videos.

matcher-type

Part of the SFM process involves finding image pairs (as explained in matcher-neighbors). After preemptive matching has identified possible image pairs, further computation identifies the actual image pairs. Image pairs are found by comparing their features. Given two sets features, the goal is to match each feature from the first set to a feature from the second set, trying to find those that represent the same object or point of interest in a scene.

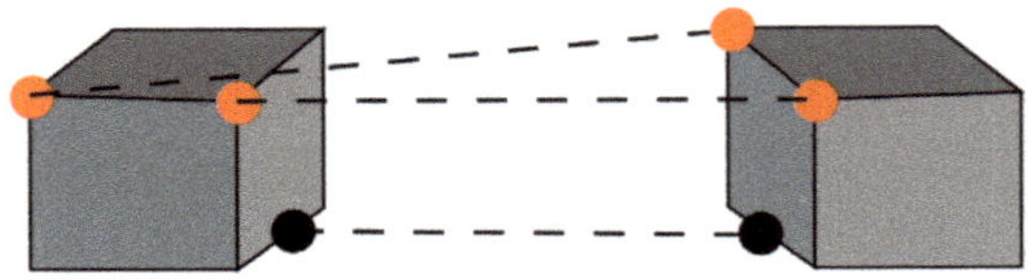

Features from one image (left) are matched to the other (right)

Note that many matches will be incorrect. That's OK, because by computing thousands of them, the program can subsequently take this mix of correct and incorrect matches and verify which ones are geometrically consistent, discarding the ones that are not.

To summarize, image matching is a multi-step process:

1. Preemptive matching (controlled via matcher-neighbors)
2. Feature matching
3. Geometric (robust) matching

Since feature matching potentially involves dozen of thousands of features per image, some algorithms have been written to avoid performing a naive brute force comparison.

Option	Search For Similar Features With
flann	An index powered by the Fast Library for Approximate Nearest Neighbors
bow	A Bag Of Words[22] approach
bruteforce	Simple brute force

[22]Bag-of-words model in computer vision: en.wikipedia.org/wiki/Bag-of-words_model_in_computer_vision

The default **flann** is the most versatile method, offering an excellent tradeoff between accuracy and speed; **bow** is faster but works only with HAHOG features and might miss some matches; **bruteforce** is slow as it exhaustively tries to match all features, but is more robust.

max-concurrency

By default the program will attempt to use all available CPU resources. There are scenarios where this might not be desirable, for example on shared servers or when there's a need to use the computer for other tasks while processing. This option limits the maximum number of CPU cores that will be used at the same time.

merge

This option controls what assets should be merged during the merge step of the split-merge pipeline. By default all available assets are merged, but users can choose to merge only specific ones. We cover this option in more detail in the Processing Large Datasets chapter.

mesh-octree-depth

When it comes to generating 3D models, this is probably the most important option. It specifies a key variable for the Screened Poisson Reconstruction[23] algorithm, which is responsible for generating a mesh from the point cloud.

[23] Screened Poisson Reconstruction: watertight surfaces from oriented point sets. cs.jhu.edu/~misha/MyPapers/ToG13.pdf

The details of the algorithm are fascinating, but probably outside the scope of this book.

To understand how this option affects the output, it helps to visually understand the concept of an octree. First, octree means *eight-tree* (okta is *eight* in Greek). Why eight? Because at each level (or *depth*) of the tree, each box (or *node or branch*) of the tree is divided in eight parts. At the first level there's only one branch. At the second level there's 8. At the third there's 64 and so forth.

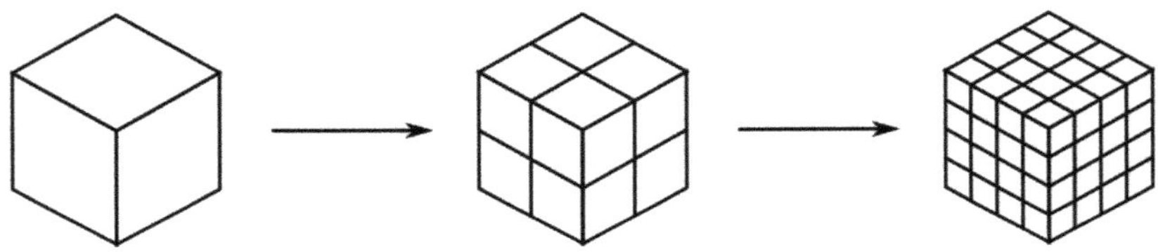

An octree with depth 1, 2 and 3

Lower depths in an octree allow finer details to be captured.

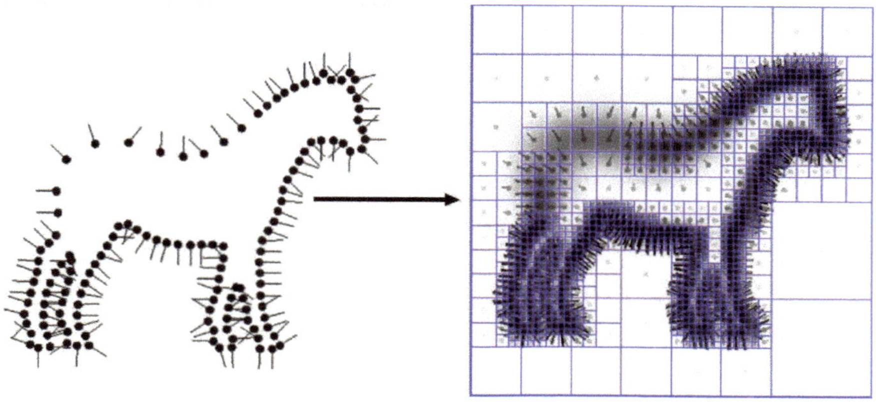

Points and resulting octree. Image from http://cs.jhu.edu/~misha/Code/

The practical aspect of this option is that the higher the value, the finer the resulting mesh will be. The trade-off is exponentially longer run-time and memory usage. The default value of 11 works well for a lot of different cases. Flat areas can benefit from lower values (6-8) and urban areas can improve by setting this value higher (12). When increasing this option, mesh-size should also be increased as finer meshes require more triangles.

mesh-octree-depth 6 and mesh-size 10000 (top) vs. mesh-octree-depth 11 and mesh-size 1000000 (bottom)

mesh-size

To keep memory usage and run-time under control, after a mesh is generated the program simplifies it by setting an upper limit to the number of triangles the mesh can contain. The more triangles a mesh contains, the longer it takes to process it in subsequent steps of the pipeline. A low triangle count can sometimes degrade the quality of the mesh. If details seem to be missing from the 3D model, increasing this option can improve results. This is especially beneficial in urban areas where buildings require fine details for more appealing results.

Effects of reducing the number of triangles in a mesh. Image courtesy of Trevorgoodchild, Quadric error metric simplification applied to the Stanford bunny, CC BY-SA 3.0

min-num-features

During the SFM process, features are extracted from the input images. This option controls the minimum number of features the program tries to find in each image, thus increasing the likelihood of finding matches between images. It does so by progressively lowering certain threshold values, which lead to more, but less ideal features.

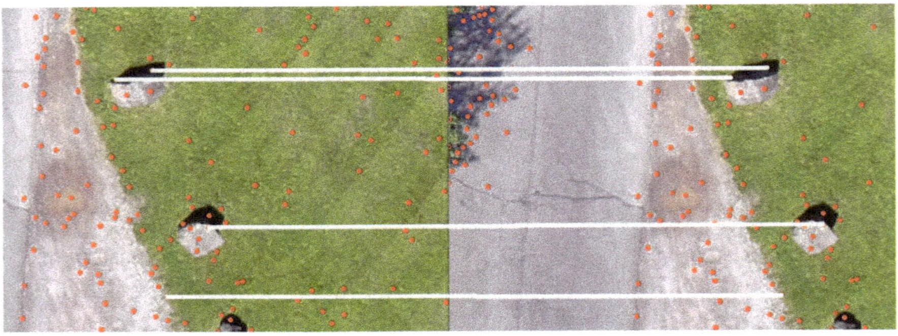

Features (red points) and matches between overlapping images (white lines). min-num-features controls the desired number of red points in each image

This option should be increased when trying to map areas that have few distinguishable features, such as forest areas:

Can you easily find many good features / reference points in the image above? Neither can a computer. But increasing the number of features can increase the likelyhood of a match between images

Increasing this option results in longer run-time, but increases the chances that a reconstruction will succeed. In certain instances, the program might also be able to generate only a partial reconstruction. In such cases users will notice that some areas for which images exists do not appear in the final results (a chunk of the orthophoto will appear to be missing). Increasing this option can help generate more complete reconstructions.

An interesting effect is that increasing this option also increases the number of points in the sparse point cloud, so it can be used in conjunction with fast-orthophoto to produce slightly better results.

no-gpu

When setup correctly, if available, a graphics card (GPU) is used to speed-up some computations. This option prevents the use of a GPU, falling back to CPU processing. We cover more details on this in the GPU Processing chapter.

optimize-disk-space

During processing several intermediate files are generated. These files can consume a lot of disk space. Turning on this option will delete these intermediate files as soon as they are no longer needed, reducing the amount of disk space needed by the process. A side effect of using this option is that you will no longer be able to restart processing from the middle of the pipeline.

orthophoto-compression

Compression is a method to save space in exchange for slightly longer run-time. The possible values for this option are:

Option	Description
DEFLATE	Also known as ZIP compression, deflate is a lossless compression method. It tends to yield slightly smaller file sizes when compared to LZW.
JPEG	Uses JPEG compression with quality value of 75. JPEG is a lossy compression method, meaning some image quality is lost during compression.

Option	Description
LZW	Uses Lempel–Ziv–Welch compression. This is a lossless compression method, meaning image quality is not lost during compression.
PACKBITS	This compression method, like LZW, is lossless. It's arguably more supported than LZW, but achieves less compression than LZW.
LZMA	Another lossless compression method.
NONE	Skips compression. Speeds up the generation of the orthophoto, but creates much larger files.

The default is **DEFLATE**.

In WebODM this option is hidden and the compression is always set to **DEFLATE**.

orthophoto-cutline

By turning on this option the program will generate a cutline. A cutline is a polygon within the orthophoto's crop area that attempts to follow the edges of features.

Cutline

Cutline going around the edges of a car

A cutline can be used to merge overlapping orthophotos by minimizing the color differences between seams. It's used to merge orthophotos when processing large datasets using the split-merge pipeline (see the Processing Large Datasets chapter).

The cutline is saved in *odm_orthophoto/cutline.gpkg*.

orthophoto-kmz

Exports the orthophoto as a Google Earth KMZ file and stores it in *odm_orthophoto/odm_orthophoto.kmz*.

This option is hidden in WebODM, as WebODM can export KMZ files on-demand.

orthophoto-no-tiled

By default the program will generate tiled TIFFs, with a tile size of 256x256 pixels. Tiling in this context is related to the arrangement of data in the file. Data can be arranged either in tiles or stripes. When reading and displaying an entire file, tiles and stripes are equivalent in performance, since all data must be read regardless. When accessing a subsection of the image however, for example when zooming into an area, using tiles often results in needing to read less data.

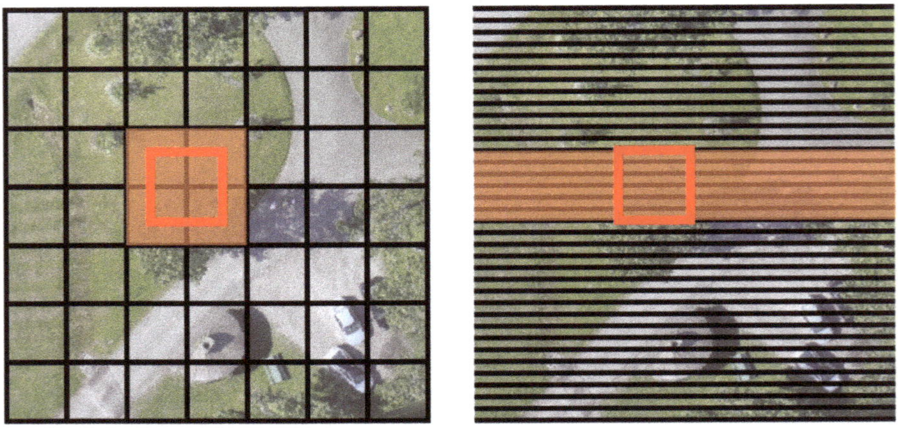

Tiles (left) vs. stripes (right). The red rectangle is the area being accessed. The highlighted area shows the amount of data that needs to be read from the file. The smaller the highlighted area, the quicker it is to access the file

Tiles are the default. Tiled orthophotos take slightly longer to create compared to striped. To use stripes, users can turn on this option.

This option is not available in WebODM.

orthophoto-png

Exports the orthophoto as a PNG file and stores it in *odm_orthophoto/odm_orthophoto.png*.

This option is hidden in WebODM, as WebODM can export PNG files on-demand.

orthophoto-resolution

This option specifies the output resolution of the orthophoto in cm / pixel. See dem-resolution, for a discussion on resolution values.

pc-classify

Points in a point cloud can be assigned one of several classification values[24] to indicate whether a point is part of the terrain (ground), of a building, of a tree (vegetation) or of other many possible classifications. By default every point is simply labeled as *unclassified* and the software does not attempt to label what each point represents. By turning on this option, a Simple Morphological Filter[25] (SMRF) is used to find the points that are part of the terrain (ground) and assign to them a ground classification value. The rest of the (non-ground) points is then evaluated using an AI classifier [26] to further identify vegetation, buildings and other man-made structures. The end result is a classified point cloud.

[24] LAS 1.4 Specification: asprs.org/wp-content/uploads/2010/12/LAS_1_4_r13.pdf

[25] SMRF: A Simple Morphological Filter for Ground Identification of LIDAR Data. github.com/thomaspingel/smrf

[26] OpenPointClass: Fast and memory efficient semantic segmentation of 3D point clouds. github.com/uav4geo/openpointclass

Point cloud (top) and classification results (bottom)

The SMRF algorithm can be controlled via four options. It's usually recommended to try the default values, examine results and then make tweaks as needed.

Option	Description
smrf-scalar	Used to make the threshold parameter dependent on the slope. To improve results, this value can be decreased slightly if the **smrf-threshold** value is increased and vice-versa.
smrf-slope	Should be set to the *largest common terrain slope*, expressed as a ratio between change in elevation and change in horizontal distance (if elevation changes by 1.5 meters over a 10 meter distance, that's 1.5 / 10 = 0.15). It should be increased for terrains with large slope variation (hills, mountains) and decreased for flat areas. For best results it should be higher than 0.1, but not higher than 1.2
smrf-threshold	Specifies the minimum height (in meters) of non-ground objects. For example, setting a value of 5 will likely be sufficient to identify buildings, but will not be sufficient to identify cars. To identify cars the value should be lowered to 2 or even 1.5 (the average car height). This parameter alone has the biggest impact on results.
smrf-window	Should be set to the size of the largest non-ground feature (in meters). For example, if a scene is full of small objects (trees), this value can be decreased. If the scene contains large objects (buildings), this value can be increased. It's recommended to keep this value above 10.

SMRF has limitations and it's important to understand them. In particular, the filter will sometimes mistakenly classify points that belong to buildings or trees as ground points (type II errors).

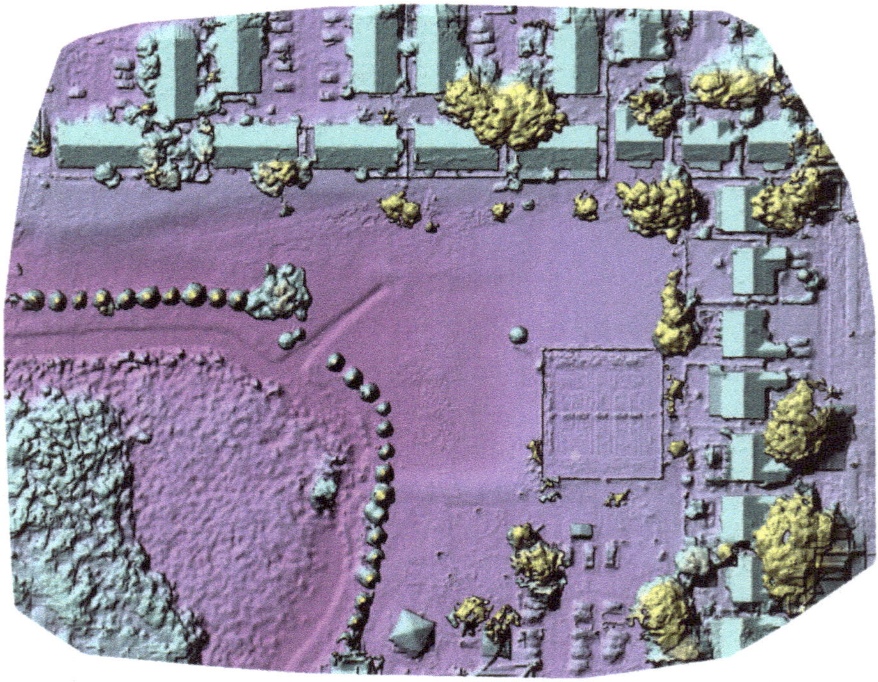

Input surface model

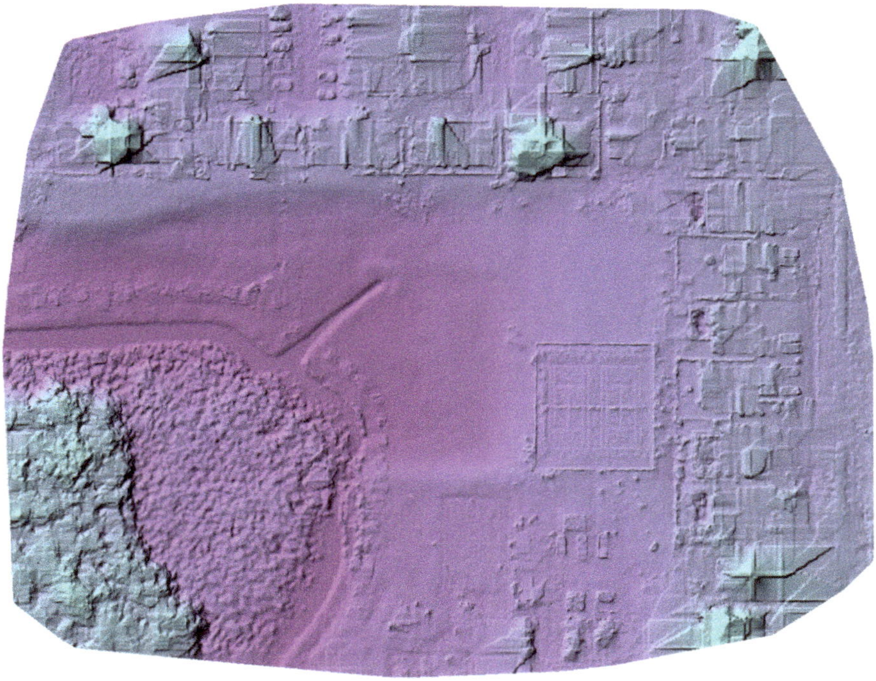

Terrain model obtained with default SMRF options. Note some houses were mistakenly included and artifacts are lingering around the edges of removed objects

A much improved terrain model obtained by setting smrf-threshold 0.3 (decreased), smrf-scalar 1.3 (increased), smrf-slope 0.05 (decreased) and smrf-window 24 (increased)

Automated methods for reliable classification of point clouds are an active area of research. SMRF performs remarkably well, but often requires some tweaking. Users wishing to generate high quality DTMs should always double check the results and adjust the SMRF options as needed. Error rates in the 10-20% range for classification of non-ground points from the AI process are also to be expected.

It's also sometimes worth comparing the classification results with those obtained from supervised or trained classification methods. CloudCompare[27] is a free and open source software that implements such methods[28].

pc-copc

Generates a Cloud Optimized Point Cloud (COPC[29]), which is stored in *odm_georeferencing/odm_georeferenced_model.copc.laz*. COPC files are simple LAZ files with an internal structure that makes them efficient to access remotely (for example when hosting them on a web server). You can view COPC files by using a viewer such as eptium.com.

This option is hidden in WebODM.

pc-csv

By default the output point cloud is exported in a compressed LAZ format. The LAZ format is not human readable and cannot be opened with a simple text editor. Users can export a copy of the point cloud to CSV (Comma Separated Values) format by turning on this option. The CSV file format is not ideal for point cloud data, but can sometimes be useful for debugging the values of the point cloud or for import in programs that do not understand LAS/LAZ. The resulting point cloud is stored in *odm_georeferencing/odm_georeferenced_model.csv*.

This option is hidden in WebODM.

---

[27] CloudCompare: cloudcompare.org
[28] CANUPO Plugin: cloudcompare.org/doc/wiki/index.php?title=CANUPO_(plugin)
[29] COPC: copc.io

pc-ept

By setting this option users can export the point cloud in Entwine Point Tile (EPT) format[30], which can be used to efficiently stream point clouds across networks (similar to COPC[31]). EPT datasets can also be efficiently analyzed, queried and transformed using tools such as PDAL[32]. The resulting EPT dataset is stored in the *entwine_pointcloud* directory*.

In WebODM this option is always turned on and it's hidden from the list.

pc-filter

Noise from the point cloud can be partially removed using a combination of statistical and visibility filtering. This option sets the standard deviation threshold value for the statistical filter. In this context standard deviation is a measure of how spread out points are relative to their neighbors. The filter looks at the closest 16 neighbors for each point and computes their standard deviations, which gives a measure of how far each point deviates from the average distance to each other point. If a point is found to be too far away relative to its neighbors, thus having a standard deviation higher than the threshold, the point is labeled as an outlier.

[30] Entwine Point Tile: entwine.io/en/latest/entwine-point-tile.html
[31] COPC: copc.io
[32] PDAL: pdal.io

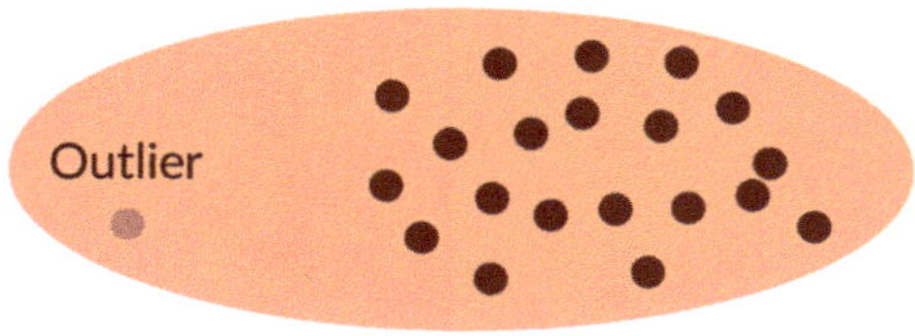

The gray point has a high standard deviation, so it's labeled as an outlier

Setting this value too high will keep some noisy points, while setting this value too low will possibly remove valid points. Filtering can be disabled by setting this option to zero.

pc-las

By default the output point cloud is exported in a compressed LAZ format. Since not all programs support LAZ, users can export a copy of the point cloud in uncompressed LAS format by turning on this option. The resulting point cloud is stored in *odm_georeferencing/odm_georeferenced_model.las*.

This option is hidden in WebODM, as WebODM can export LAS files on-demand.

pc-quality

During MVS, this option defines the resolution of the depthmap images that are computed, which affects the density of the resulting point cloud. A depthmap is an image containing information relative to the distance of objects in a scene.

Image and corresponding depthmap. Darker areas are closer to the camera.
Image courtesy of Dominicus, Cubic Structure, CC BY-SA 3.0

Higher resolution depthmaps increase the number of points, but can also increase the amount of noise. Increasing the depthmap resolution will increase run-time quadratically (twice the resolution will take 4x the time to compute). If you need to change the density of your point clouds, this is the option to tweak. Point clouds are the basis for 3D models, which in turn are used to generate orthophotos. When mapping urban areas, if the buildings contain holes, look malformed or "wavy", a higher density point cloud could help obtain better looking results. Increasing this value too much can increase noise, so there's a subtle balance between point density and quality of results. The memory and run-time requirements are also factors that should be considered when changing this option.

Each option corresponds to a scaling factor:

Option	Scaling Factor
ultra	1/2
high	1/4

Option	Scaling Factor
medium	1/8
low	1/16
lowest	1/32

Different image dimensions also correspond to a multiplier value:

Largest Image Dimension (megapixels)	Multiplier
< 6	2x
6 - 42	1
> 42	1/2

The depthmap resolution is then calculated with:

```
depthmap_resolution = max(320, max_image_dimension *
  ↪ scaling_factor * multiplier)
```

For example, a dataset with 4000x3000 (12 megapixels) images and this option set to **high** will compute depthmaps at 1000 pixels.

```
image = (4000,3000)
max_image_dimension = max(image) # <-- 4000
megapixels = image[0]*image[1]/1000000 # <-- 12
multiplier = 1 # From table
scaling_factor = 1/4 # pc-quality: high
print(max(320, max_image_dimension * scaling_factor *
  ↪ multiplier)) # <-- 1000 pixels
```

Note that depthmap resolution is never allowed to be lower than 320 pixels.

pc-sample

This option sets an upper limit on the density of the dense point cloud, expressed as a radius in meters under which no two points should exist. For example, a value of 0.01 filters the point cloud such that points are no closer than 1 centimeter (0.01 meters) from each other. It can be useful for reducing memory usage and processing speed, or for achieving a specific point cloud density target.

pc-skip-geometric

During MVS, a geometric refinement process is used to improve the depthmaps and the resulting point cloud. This process can take some time and can be skipped by using this option.

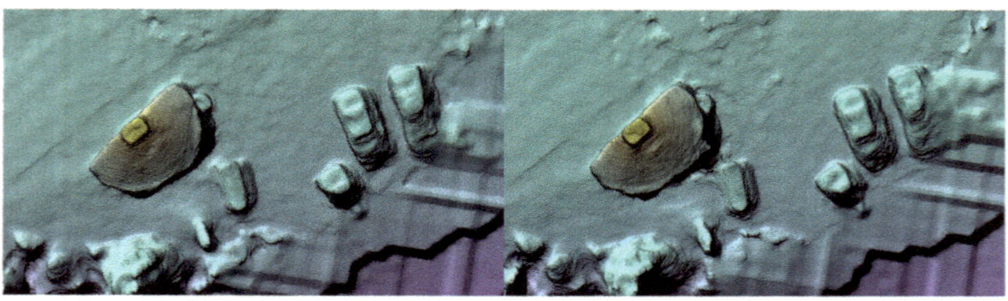

Elevation model computed with defaults (left) vs. computed with pc-skip-geometric (right). Note the building and cars are better defined on the left

primary-band

This option specifies the band name (Red, Blue, Green, NIR, etc.) to use for reconstructing multispectral datasets. The name of the band must match the one found in the EXIF tags of the images. Only the images part of this band will be used for 3D reconstruction. We cover this option more in details in the Multispectral Datasets chapter.

Setting a value of **auto** (the default) chooses the band with the smallest band index number, which is also specified in the EXIF tags.

project-path

When using ODX from the command line, this option sets the path where projects are stored.

```
projects/          <-- project-path
|-- a              <-- dataset name
|    |-- images
|-- b              <-- dataset name
     |-- images
```

We cover this option more in detail in The Command Line chapter. This option is not available in WebODM.

radiometric-calibration

Radiometric calibration is the ability to convert pixel values (digital numbers) to reflectance. ODX can automatically perform radiometric calibration and calculate both reflectance and temperature values for a variety of sensors[33].

Option	Description
none	No radiometric calibration (digital number outputs)
camera	Applies black level, vignetting, gain and exposure corrections using information from the EXIF tags. Also computes absolute temperature values when appropriate.
camera+sun	Same as **camera**, but also applies corrections from a downwelling light sensor (DLS) if available.

We cover this option in more detail in the Multispectral Datasets chapter.

rerun

Shorthand for rerun-from **<step>** end-with **<step>**.

rerun-all

Shorthand for rerun-from **dataset**, while also removing all output folders before starting the process.

rerun-from

Same as end-with, except that it instructs the program to resume execution from a specific point in the pipeline, skipping previous steps.

[33] Supported Multispectral Hardware: docs.webodm.org/multispectral/#supported-sensors

When using WebODM the rerun-from option is automatically set when using the **Restart** button dropdown.

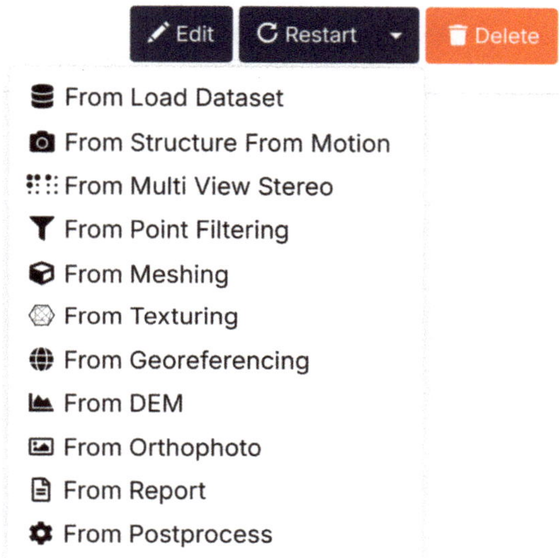

Restart drop-down in WebODM

It's not always possible to restart a task from a certain step in WebODM. The processing node must support task restarts and the task's intermediate results need to have been kept on disk (by default they are kept only for 2 days). See The NodeODX API chapter for information on how to change the number of days results are kept. Tasks also cannot be restarted from a certain step if the optimize-disk-space option has been used.

rolling-shutter

Enables rolling shutter correction, which can help increase reconstruction accuracy when datasets are captured with rolling shutter sensors. We cover this option in more detail in the Rolling Shutter Correction chapter.

rolling-shutter-readout

Overrides the default sensor readout time value used for rolling shutter correction. We cover this option in more detail in the Rolling Shutter Correction chapter.

sfm-algorithm

The SFM process supports three different methods to reconstruct a scene:

Option	Description
incremental	The default. General purpose. Works with all scenes and supports multiple cameras. Cameras are added to the reconstruction incrementally, step-by-step. Most reliable.
triangulation	If gimbal angles and GPS information is available, camera positions are initialized from those values in one step and iteratively refined. It can sometimes generate better results and can process a bit faster than **incremental**. It's experimental and does not work with all cameras.

Option	Description
planar	If the scene is flat (e.g. a farm field), captured with a single camera, at a constant altitude and with the camera pointed straight down (nadir), then you should use this option. It will process 5-10x times faster than **incremental**. It works with multispectral datasets also.

sfm-no-partial

If there are any gaps in overlap or insufficient good features between images, the SFM process will generate two or more separate (partial) reconstructions. By default if GPS information is available, ODX will *attempt* to merge such reconstructions into one. This does not always work due to the fact that the reconstructions no longer share a common coordinate system.

This option instructs ODX to never merge partial reconstructions and to use the one with the largest amount of images while dropping the others.

skip-3dmodel

Sometimes all that a user wants is an orthophoto. In that case, it's not necessary to generate a full 3D model. This option saves some time by skipping the commands that produce a 3D model. A 2.5D model (a 3D model where elevation is simply *extruded* from the ground plane) is still generated. 2.5D models are not *true* 3D models as they cannot represent the true shape of objects such as overhangs, but work well for the purpose of rendering orthophotos.

3D model (top) vs. 2.5D model (bottom). Note the absence of overhangs in the bottom image

By default both models are created. See also use-3dmesh.

skip-band-alignment

When capturing multispectral images, typically the camera sensors for each band are slightly offset from one another. This causes small misalignments between image bands. ODX performs automatic band alignment as part of its multispectral processing pipeline. If a person has manually performed image alignment using other software, automatic alignment can be disabled by using this option.

We cover this option in more detail in the Multispectral Datasets chapter.

skip-orthophoto

If an orthophoto is not needed, this option can save you some time by skipping the orthophoto generation step.

skip-report

If a PDF report is not needed, this option can save you some time by skipping the report generation step.

sky-removal

Uses artificial intelligence methods to automatically generate image masks that remove the sky. This is useful for processing datasets that have parts of the sky, perhaps due to oblique images needed to capture 3D structures. Sky areas tend to generate noise in the resulting 3D model and this option helps in removing most of it.

3D point cloud without (top) and with sky masks (bottom). Sceaux castle model generated from photos by Pierre Moulon[34]

See also the image masks chapter.

[34]Sceaux castle: github.com/openMVG/ImageDataset_SceauxCastle

sm-cluster

Specifies a URL to a ClusterODX instance. When combined with the split option, it enables the distributed split-merge pipeline for processing large datasets in parallel using multiple processing nodes. We cover this option in more detail in the Processing Large Datasets chapter.

sm-no-align

During split-merge, the entire model is split into parts (submodels). The submodels at some point need to be aligned to each other. The alignment is performed by minimizing the differences in camera positions and orientations between overlapping areas.

In certain cases, such as when high precision GPS information is available, it can be better to skip this alignment step and to rely on the GPS information to keep the submodels aligned.

smrf-scalar

Controls the scalar variable for SMRF. See pc-classify.

smrf-slope

Controls the slope variable for SMRF. See pc-classify.

smrf-threshold

Controls the threshold variable for SMRF. See pc-classify.

smrf-window

Controls the window variable for SMRF. See pc-classify.

split

When set to a number lower than the number of input images, enables the split-merge pipeline. We cover this option in more detail in the Processing Large Datasets chapter.

split-image-groups

By default ODX looks for a file named **image_groups.txt** in the project directory. If it exists, it's used to manually specify how a dataset should be split into parts when processing it using split-merge. We cover this option in more detail in the Processing Large Datasets chapter.

This option is not shown in WebODM and is automatically set if a file named **image_groups.txt** is uploaded with a dataset.

split-overlap

Specifies the amount of overlap (in meters) that submodels should have during the split-merge pipeline. We cover this option in more detail in the

Processing Large Datasets chapter.

texturing-keep-unseen-faces

The input to the texturing part of the pipeline consists of a mesh, cameras and images. The input mesh is composed of triangles. The program at some point checks which triangles are visible by the cameras. By default if a triangle is not visible by any camera, it's discarded from the output.

Unseen faces are removed from the textured mesh (top) vs. faces are kept with no color (bottom)

This option instructs the program to keep all triangles, regardless of whether they are seen by a camera or not.

texturing-single-material

The 3D models generated by ODX are in Wavefront OBJ[35] format. This format allows the storage of color information to be saved across multiple image files (textures). Each texture in the model is associated to a “material”. ODX by default uses multiple materials and textures when generating OBJ files. Some programs have difficulties opening OBJs with multiple materials, or certain operations on multi-material mesh can be complex. For example when editing the mesh in a program such as Blender[36].

Using this option will generate an OBJ with a single material, at the expense of slightly longer runtime.

texturing-skip-global-seam-leveling

During texturing the program needs to merge together images that have strong color differences, due to illumination and exposure differences.

[35] Wavefront OBJ: en.wikipedia.org/wiki/Wavefront_.obj_file
[36] Blender: blender.org

Seams in the textured model due to different illumination (top) and global seam leveling applied (bottom)

This kind of adjustment is referred to as *global* because it's computed on all images at once. The goal is to minimize the difference between the images as to achieve consistent luminosity throughout.

Global seam leveling affects reflectance/temperature values when processing multispectral datasets and it might be desirable to enable this option to turn it off.

tiles

This option generates static TMS[37] tiles for orthophotos and DEMs. TMS tiles can be useful for hosting/sharing maps on a website and are compatible with many viewers such as Leaflet[38]. The DEM tiles are generated using a colored hillshade style. The resulting tiles are stored in the *orthophoto_tiles*, *dsm_tiles* and *dtm_tiles* folders.

In WebODM buttons to download the tiles will appear when clicking the *Download* button.

use-3dmesh

By default a 2.5D textured mesh is used to render the orthophoto. 2.5D meshes tend to work well for most aerial datasets, but can sometimes lead to subpar results, especially if there are no nadir images in the datasets (images with the camera pointed straight or almost straight at the ground). The reason for it is that the texturing step is performed differently between 3D and 2.5D meshes. 2.5D meshes give priority to nadir images, and if these are missing, the

[37] TMS: Tile Map Service: wiki.openstreetmap.org/wiki/TMS
[38] Leaflet: leafletjs.com

texturing might be of lesser quality compared to a 3D mesh. For points of interests, such as one obtained by orbiting a single building at close range with oblique images, a 2.5D mesh will also perform poorly. This option instructs the program to use the full 3D model for generating an orthophoto and to skip the generation of the 2.5D model. See also skip-3dmodel.

use-exif

A Ground Control Point file will always be used if either a *gcp_list.txt* file exists in the project directory (ODX) or if a GCP file has been uploaded with a dataset (WebODM). By turning on this option, the program ignores the GCP file and relies on the location information from the images' EXIF tags instead.

use-fixed-camera-params

During the SFM process, the camera's internal parameters (focal length, optical center, etc.) need to be estimated and refined to achieve a good reconstruction. Sometimes, due to poor image collection practices, the camera parameters are wrongly estimated and can result in reconstructions that exhibit a *doming* effect. While better solutions to the doming effect are explained in the Camera Calibration chapter and through the use of the cameras option, by turning on this option it's possible to instruct the software not to optimize camera parameters at all (keeping the parameters fixed). This can sometimes improve results if there's little to no geometric distortion in the images and the focal length value embedded in the images' EXIF tags is accurate.

use-hybrid-bundle-adjustment

Bundle adjustment (BA) is a refinement step during the SFM process that improves the position/orientation of cameras, 3D points and camera parameters. This process needs to be done at regular intervals during the reconstruction to avoid the accumulation of errors, but is also computationally expensive. It comes in two varieties, local and global. Local BA only refines a subset of the reconstruction, whereas global BA refines the entire reconstruction. Performing global bundle adjustment requires re-evaluating the entire scene. By default, the program will perform global BA after the number of new triangulated points in the scene has increased by 20% and will never perform local BA.

By turning on this option, the program changes the logic that triggers global BA and enables local BA. A global BA is forced every time 100 new cameras are added to the scene, regardless of the number of new points added to the reconstruction and local BA is performed at regular intervals by optimizing together cameras that share at least one image pair. In short, this option increases the number of times that bundle adjustment is performed.

Turning on this option increases the total run-time, but can help increase the accuracy of the reconstruction and reduce doming effects.

version

This option causes the program to print the ODX version and exit. This option is not shown in WebODM. To find the ODX version number in WebODM, one can navigate to **Processing Nodes — node-odx-1**. The version will be listed under **Engine Version**.

video-limit

ODX can process video files (.mp4, .mov, .lrv and .ts) by extracting image frames at regular intervals. The program will automatically filter out blurry and dark frames. For DJI drones, if a subtitle (.srt) file is available, it will be used to add GPS information to the extracted images. When using a subtitle file, it needs to match the filename of the video. For example, **video.mp4** should have a corresponding **video.srt** file (case sensitive).

This option sets the number of images that should be extracted from the video files. The default is 500.

video-resolution

Sets the resolution of the images extracted from video files. For example, if a video file has a resolution of 3840x2160 pixels and this option is set to 2000, the extracted images will have a resolution of 2000x1125 pixels.

See also video-limit.

Changing Options and Restarting

If you need to change an option, often times you don't need to restart a task from the very beginning. Instead you can restart from an intermediate stage (see rerun-from). The table below lists the appropriate stage to restart from when changing an option:

Option	Restart Stage
3d-tiles	PostProcess
align	Georeferencing
auto-boundary	Point Filtering
auto-boundary-distance	Point Filtering
bg-removal	Load Dataset
boundary	Point Filtering
build-overviews	Orthophoto
camera-lens	Load Dataset
cameras	Load Dataset
cog	DEM
copy-to	PostProcess
crop	Georeferencing
dem-decimation	DEM
dem-euclidean-map	DEM
dem-gapfill-steps	DEM
dem-resolution	DEM
dsm	DEM
dtm	DEM
end-with	N/A
fast-orthophoto	Point Filtering
feature-quality	Structure From Motion

Option	Restart Stage
feature-type	Structure From Motion
force-gps	Structure From Motion
gcp	Load Dataset
geo	Load Dataset
gltf	PostProcess
gps-accuracy	Load Dataset
gps-z-offset	Load Dataset
help	N/A
ignore-gsd	Structure From Motion
matcher-neighbors	Structure From Motion
matcher-order	Structure From Motion
matcher-type	Structure From Motion
max-concurrency	N/A
merge	Merge
mesh-octree-depth	Meshing
mesh-size	Meshing
min-num-features	Structure From Motion
no-gpu	N/A
optimize-disk-space	N/A
orthophoto-compression	Orthophoto
orthophoto-cutline	Orthophoto

Option	Restart Stage
orthophoto-kmz	Orthophoto
orthophoto-no-tiled	Orthophoto
orthophoto-png	Orthophoto
orthophoto-resolution	Orthophoto
pc-classify	DEM
pc-copc	Georeferencing
pc-csv	Georeferencing
pc-ept	Georeferencing
pc-filter	Multi View Stereo
pc-las	Georeferencing
pc-quality	Structure From Motion
pc-sample	Point Filtering
pc-skip-geometric	Multi View Stereo
primary-band	Load Dataset
project-path	N/A
radiometric-calibration	Structure From Motion
rerun	N/A
rerun-all	N/A
rerun-from	N/A
rolling-shutter	Structure From Motion
rolling-shutter-readout	Structure From Motion

Option	Restart Stage
sfm-algorithm	Structure From Motion
sfm-no-partial	Structure From Motion
skip-3dmodel	Meshing
skip-band-alignment	Structure From Motion
skip-orthophoto	Orthophoto
skip-report	Report
sky-removal	Load Dataset
sm-cluster	Split
sm-no-align	Split
smrf-scalar	DEM
smrf-slope	DEM
smrf-threshold	DEM
smrf-window	DEM
split	Split
split-image-groups	Split
split-overlap	Split
texturing-keep-unseen-faces	Texturing
texturing-single-material	Texturing
texturing-skip-global-seam-leveling	Texturing
tiles	DEM
use-3dmesh	Texturing

Option	Restart Stage
use-exif	Load Dataset
use-fixed-camera-params	Structure From Motion
use-hybrid-bundle-adjustment	Structure From Motion
version	N/A
video-limit	Load Dataset
video-resolution	Load Dataset

7. Ground Control Points

A ground control point (GCP) is a position measurement made on the ground, typically using a high precision GPS[1]. Measurements are made near identifiable structures such as street corners or by placing visible markers on the terrain.

[1] I use GPS as a synonym for GNSS, for simplicity.

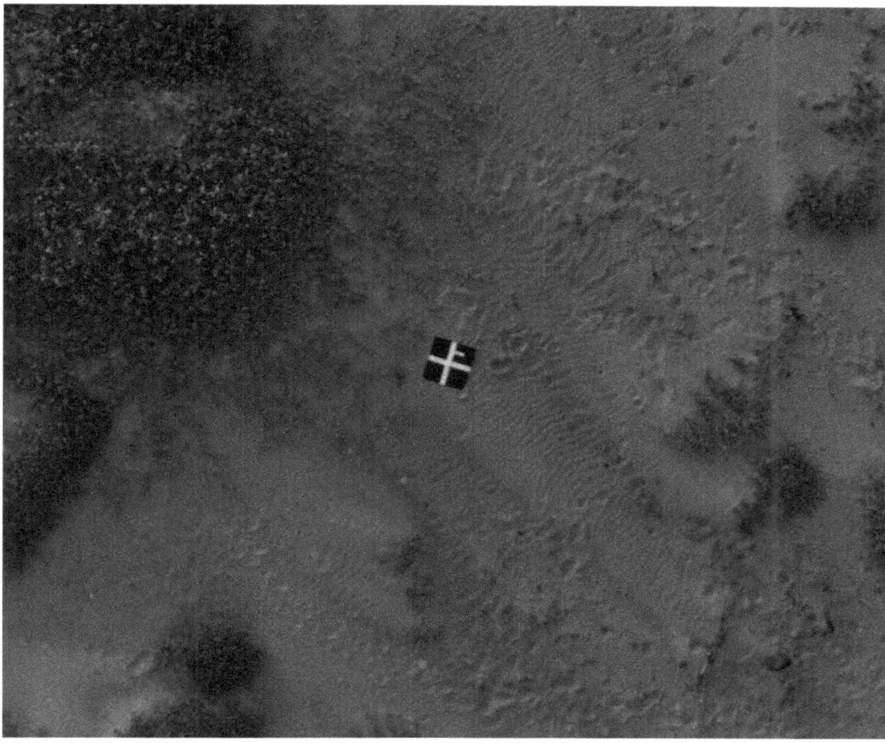

A ground control point marker. Image courtesy of Michele M. Tobias & Alex Mandel Creative Commons Attribution-ShareAlike 4.0 International CC BY-SA 4.0

Images that contain the visible markers can then be *tagged* by creating a correspondence between the image location of the markers and their real world positions.

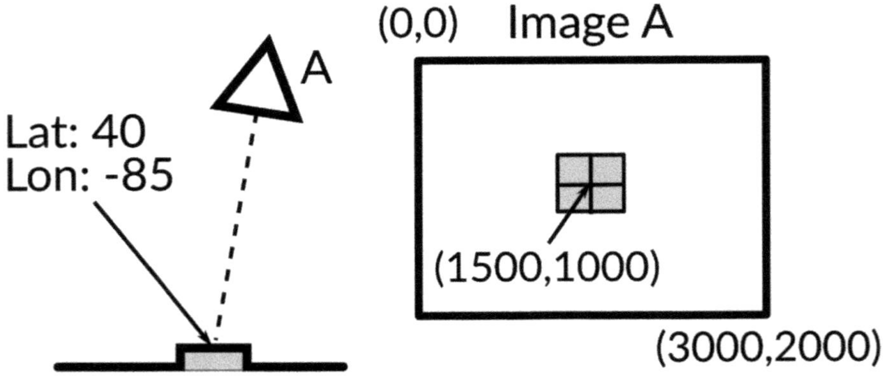

A GCP marker is photographed by camera A to produce Image A. In a second step, the pixel location of the marker (1500,1000) from Image A can be manually tagged with its real world coordinates (latitude 40, longitude -85)

Using ground control points can increase the georeferencing accuracy of a reconstruction, since measurements of static (non-moving) objects using a high precision GPS are often better than those obtained from the GPS of moving UAVs.

The ideal number of ground control points ranges between 5 to 8, placed evenly across the area to be flown. Adding more than 8 ground control points does not necessarily result in increased accuracy.

If the same marker is visible from multiple images, it should be tagged multiple times for each image. Ideally each marker should be tagged at least 3 times. Another way to think of it is to capture each marker on at least 3 images. This is so that the marker's location can be triangulated during computation.

Ground control points can be used by providing an additional text file along with the input images. The file follows a simple format:

The first line indicates the spatial reference system (SRS) of the world coordinates. There are no restrictions on the type of SRS you can use. Internally the program will convert the coordinates to the nearest WGS84 UTM[2] projection. The SRS can be specified using three different formats:

1) WGS84 UTM *zone number|hemisphere*
2) EPSG:*code*
3) *proj4*

Format #1 is just a human readable format specifying a UTM projection using the WGS84 reference ellipsoid and datum. Format #2 uses EPSG codes[3], which are a standard to reference many common spatial reference systems. Format #3 uses Proj4 strings[4] , which are used to explicitly to define spatial reference systems. Format #1 and #2 are preferred over #3.

These are all valid examples of SRS definitions for a GCP file:

```
WGS84 UTM 16N
WGS84 UTM 32S
EPSG:4326
EPSG:32616
+proj=longlat +ellps=WGS84 +datum=WGS84 +no_defs
```

A great resource to lookup spatial reference systems and their definitions is spatialreference.org.

The next lines in the GCP file are the world X, Y, Z coordinates, associated pixel coordinates and the image filename (case sensitive). Optionally, extra fields (such as a label) can be specified after that. Tabs and spaces can be used interchangeably to separate fields.

[2]UTM: en.wikipedia.org/wiki/Universal_Transverse_Mercator_coordinate_system
[3]EPSG: epsg.org
[4]Proj Quick Start: proj.org/en/stable/usage/quickstart.html

```
spatial reference system
geo_x geo_y geo_z im_x im_y image_name [label] [extras]
geo_x geo_y geo_z im_x im_y image_name [label] [extras]
...
```

The GCP from the example image A we've shown above, for example, would be represented as:

```
EPSG:4326
-85 40 NaN 1500 1000 ImageA.jpg gcp1
```

The **geo_z** field in this case is set to *NaN* because we didn't have an altitude value.

Marking Checkpoints

Checkpoints are useful to help validate the accuracy of a reconstruction. A checkpoint is a measurement that is left out from the reconstruction process and is only used post-processing to compare its measured vs. reconstructed position.

You mark a checkpoint by prefixed its label with **CHK-**. For example:

```
EPSG:4326
-85 40 NaN 1500 1000 ImageA.jpg CHK-gcp1
```

Creating a GCP file using POSM GCPi

The task of manually finding and measuring pixel coordinates from all images and tying marker locations to world coordinates can be tedious and error prone at best.

The Portable OpenStreetMap Ground Control Point Interface (POSM GCPi) provides a way to make this process a bit easier. The application is already loaded as a default plugin in WebODM and can be accessed via the **GCP Interface** panel.

Alternatively it can also be downloaded and run as a standalone application by following the instructions on the project's home page[5]. It's also hosted online at webodm.net/gcpi.

Step 1. Create a GCP file stub

After measuring the location of your markers it's likely that you'll end up having a list of labeled point coordinates. Exporting them to CSV format and opening them in a spreadsheet application such as LibreOffice Calc[6] should yield something similar to:

```
X,Y,Z,Label
-91.9943320967465,46.8423713026218,0,gcp1
-91.9938849653384,46.8423668860772,0,gcp2
-91.9942463047423,46.8425277454029,0,gcp3
```

From here, let's add two new columns for the *px, py* fields (initialized to zero) and shift the *Label* column to the right, so that our file now looks like:

```
X,Y,Z,px,py,Label
-91.9943320967465,46.8423713026218,0,0,0,gcp1
```

[5]POSM GCPi: github.com/WebODM/posm-gcpi
[6]LibreOffice: libreoffice.org

```
-91.9938849653384,46.8423668860772,0,0,0,gcp2
-91.9942463047423,46.8425277454029,0,0,0,gcp3
```

Finally, we remove the first line, replacing it with a SRS definition and save the CSV file making sure to use *tabs* or *spaces* instead of *commas* as a separator character. In LibreOffice Calc you can achieve this by clicking **File - Save As...** and from the bottom left of the save window check **Edit Filter Settings**. The final result opened in a text editor should look like:

```
EPSG:4326
-91.9943320967465 46.8423713026218 0 0 0 gcp1
-91.9938849653384 46.8423668860772 0 0 0 gcp2
-91.9942463047423 46.8425277454029 0 0 0 gcp3
```

Step 2: Import the GCP file stub

From POSM GCPi, press the **Load existing Control Point File** button and select the file you just created in step 1. After pressing **Load** the map on the right should update to reflect the position of your points.

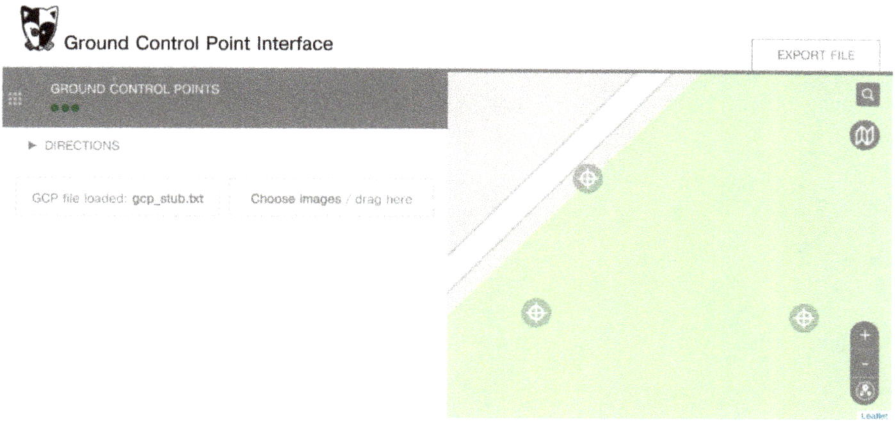

Loading a GCP stub into POSM GCPi

Step 3. Import the images and start tagging

Now import the images by pressing **Choose images**. Clicking an image will expand the panel on the left. Due to a usability quirk, the interface will add a new ground control point, which we need to remove. You can click the point on the right panel and delete it. Now from the left panel you can pan and zoom around the image to move the target icon at the location of your marker. Once it's in the proper position, simply click the target icon once from the left panel and click the corresponding target icon from the right panel. The target icon should turn green, indicating a correspondence has been set.

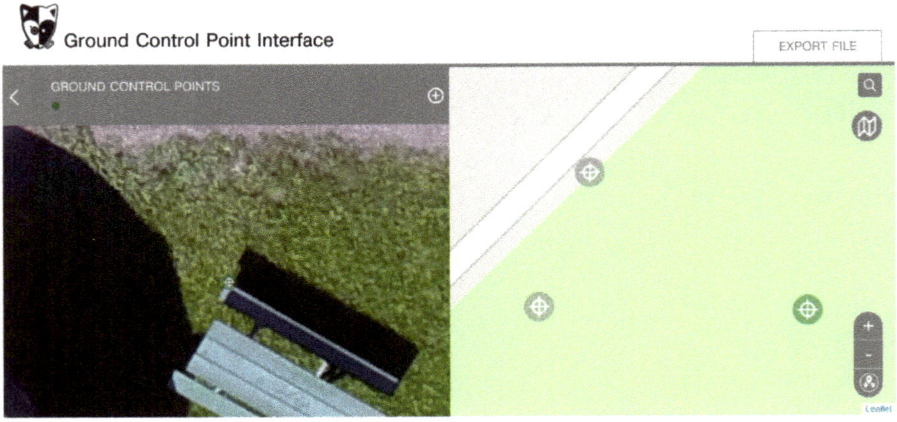

Tagging images with points using POSM GCPi

Now you can repeat the process for every marker and every image. If you get tired or want to save your work, press **Export File** and save the result in a location of your choice. You can resume your work by reloading the images and the exported file.

Notice the green dot on the top left corner. The dot shows the number of points that have been connected to at least one image (in this case, one). At the end of the process you'll want to have at least 5 or 8 green dots.

Step 4. Export the GCP file

Once you are done, you can press the **Export File** button to export your finished GCP file. This is the file that you will be using for the next steps.

Creating a GCP file using GCP Editor Pro

There's also another program for creating GCP files: GCP Editor Pro[7].

The program is released under the Fair Source License[8], which is not open source: it is available for free for one person (per organization) to use, otherwise a license needs to be purchased.

I don't cover usage of GCP Editor Pro in this book because it's not open source, but readers should be aware that it exists.

Using GCP files

With WebODM using a GCP file is as simple as including it along with the images during file selection. With ODX, the GCP file should be placed in your project folder and be named **gcp_list.txt**. Alternatively, you can use the gcp option to specify a path to a GCP file.

When a GCP file is used to process a dataset in WebODM, the position of the GCPs can be toggled from the layer list in the **Map** view:

[7]GCP Editor Pro: github.com/uav4geo/GCPEditorPro
[8]Fair Source License: fair.io

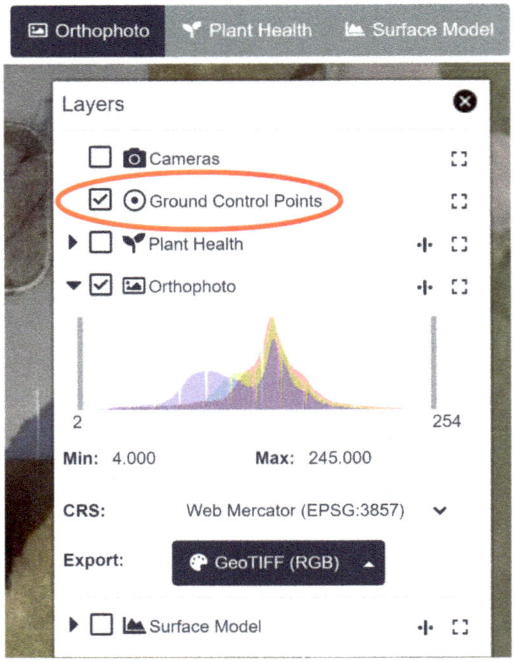

Toggling GCP markers

GCP markers are blue, while checkpoints are green. Clicking on a GCP marker on the map will also bring up a popup showing the tagged and projected location of the GCP.

This can be a useful tool to diagnose issues with GCPs and identify points that might have been tagged incorrectly, or contribute negatively to the results. A good GCP will have its tagged location pretty close to its projected location.

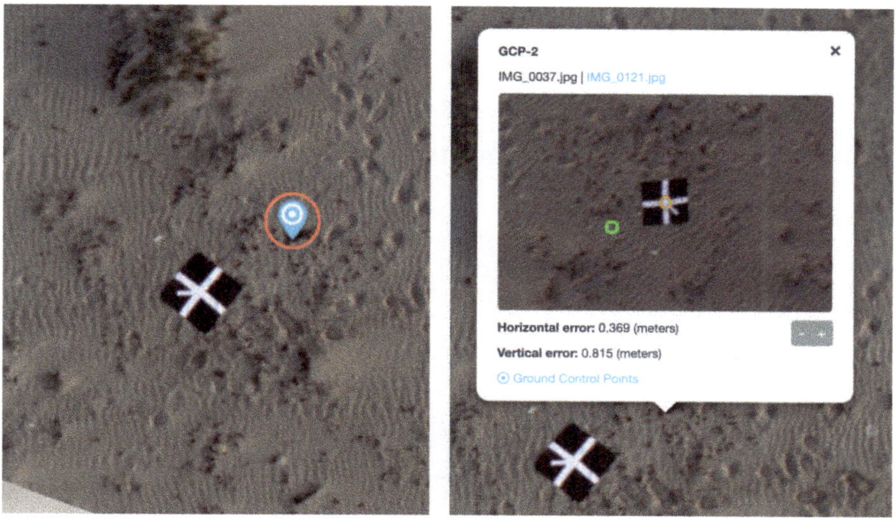

GCP marker (left) and associated popup after clicking it (right). In the example above the GCP does not fall exactly on the ground target, suggesting an issue with data collection or tagging

GCP quality metrics are also available from the PDF Report. We cover them in more detail in the Report Analysis chapter.

How GCP files work

Sometimes the final results might not align perfectly with your ground control points. It's important to understand why. GCP observations are used during the SFM step. During that step, camera positions are estimated based on an error minimization problem with many variables involved. GCP observations are used to minimize the georeferencing alignment error, but they can't compensate for other factors such as an incorrect camera model estimate due to a sub-optimal flight path or excessive camera lens distortion (see the Camera Calibration chapter). If your results do not align perfectly, first check for mistakes in your GCP file. If there are none, read and apply the concepts from the Camera Calibration chapter to improve results.

Internally ODX will always convert the coordinates of your GCP file to the nearest WGS84 / UTM CRS. For example, if your GCP coordinates are measured in central Florida, the system will reproject those coordinates to WGS 84 / UTM zone 17N[9] before processing.

Common Mistakes

The top two most common mistakes while working with GCPs are accidental swaps of X/Y axes or the choice of the wrong coordinate reference system. If points don't show up where you expect them to be on the map, check that your X/Y coordinates haven't been accidentally swapped and that you're picking the correct coordinate reference system.

[9] EPSG:32617: epsg.io/32617

8. Geolocation Files

Sometimes GPS information is available, but it's not embedded in the images. ODX provides a convenient format for associating GPS and gimbal information to images without the need to modify them.

A geolocation file (GEO) is a text file similar to ground control points files:

The first line is the spatial reference system (SRS) of the coordinates. There are no restrictions on the type of SRS you can use. Internally the program will convert the coordinates to WGS84 latitude/longitude[1]. The SRS can be specified using either:

1) EPSG:*code*
2) *proj4*

We've briefly covered EPSG codes and Proj4 strings in the Ground Control Points chapter.

These are all valid examples of SRS definitions for a GEO file:

```
EPSG:4326
+proj=longlat +ellps=WGS84 +datum=WGS84 +no_defs
```

The subsequent lines in the GEO file are the image name, X, Y, Z coordinates, yaw, pitch, roll, horizontal accuracy and vertical accuracy. Optionally, extra

[1]EPSG:4326: epsg.io/4326

fields (such as a label) can be specified after that. Tabs and spaces can be used interchangeably to separate fields.

```
spatial reference system
image x y z yaw pitch roll h_accuracy v_accuracy label
image x y z yaw pitch roll h_accuracy v_accuracy label
...
```

Only **image**, **x** and **y** are required. The other fields are optional. Yaw, pitch and roll can be set to zero if they are missing or unknown.

Here's an example of a GEO file:

```
EPSG:4326
DJI_0031.JPG    -91.99420961   46.84252125     198.609
DJI_0032.JPG    -91.99382956   46.84245844     198.609
```

Field	Description
image	Image filename (must match one of the images in the dataset)
x	Longitude/easting location of the image center
y	Latitude/northing location of the image center
z	Altitude of the image center
yaw	Yaw of the camera (degrees)
pitch	Pitch of the camera (degrees)
roll	Roll of the camera (degrees)

Field	Description
h_accuracy	GPS horizontal (X/Y) accuracy (in meters)
v_accuracy	GPS vertical (Z) accuracy (in meters)
label	Optional label

Yaw, pitch and roll (YPC[2]) values are terms that represent the orientation of the camera. They are used when sfm-algorithm is set to *triangulation* and when radiometric-calibration is set to *camera+sun*. There are no other uses for these values and they can be set to zero if you don't use these options.

It's important to note that ODX makes the assumption that the camera is attached to the drone airframe using a camera stabilizer (gimbal), with the camera oriented in such a way that the top of the image points forward relative to the airframe. This setup is very common, but it's not the only one. At the time of writing, more sophisticated configurations will not work well with ODX.

You can follow this table to set YPC values:

Field	Example	Description
yaw	0	Top of image points north
yaw	90	Top of image points east
yaw	270	Top of image points west
pitch	0	Camera points at the ground
pitch	90	Camera points at the horizon

[2]Yaw, Pitch, and Roll: simple.wikipedia.org/wiki/Pitch,_yaw,_and_roll

Field	Example	Description
roll	0	Assuming a gimbal, there's no roll

Horizontal and vertical accuracy values are used during the SFM process and should be set accordingly. If not set, the default is 10 meters.

Using GEO files

With WebODM you can use a GEO file by including it along with the images during file selection. The file must be named **geo.txt**.

With ODX, the GEO file should be placed in your project folder and also be named **geo.txt**. Alternatively, you can use the geo option to specify a path to a GEO file.

9. Multispectral Datasets

There are several sensors[1] that can simultaneously capture multiple images of different ranges (bands) of the light spectrum. The ranges often include the visible spectrum (Red, Green, Blue), near-infrared (NIR), red-edge (Re) and long-wave infrared (LWIR).

Capturing bands outside of the visible spectrum can be useful for several uses, most frequently for crop monitoring and temperature analysis.

ODX supports automatic processing, calibration and alignment of multispectral images.

Supported Images

With multispectral sensors you typically get multiple images for each individual shot, one image for each band. Some sensors combine the bands into a single file, e.g. they combine the Red, Green and Blue (RGB) bands into a single JPEG file and leave the other bands as separate files.

With the exception of the RGB bands, which can be provided either as a single file or multiple ones, ODX requires a separate file for each additional band. The files can be any of the following:

[1]Supported Multispectral Hardware: docs.webodm.org/multispectral/#supported-sensors

- JPEG (8bit)
- TIFF (8bit, 16bit and 32bit)

For TIFFs, 16bit bit TIFFs are assumed to have values between 0 and 65535 and 32bit to be single-precision floating-point numbers (numbers with decimals). QGIS[2] can be used to validate whether the images are of the correct data type. Drag and drop an image into QGIS, then from the layers list right-click the image and select **Properties... — Information**.

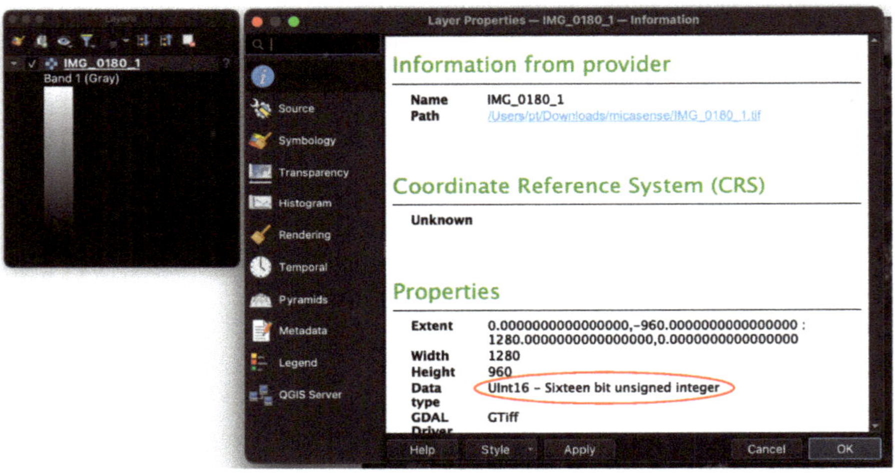

QGIS's layer properties can show the data type of any image

In QGIS the data type should be either **Byte** (8bit), **UInt16** (16bit unsigned) or **Float32** (32bit float). Other data types are not supported.

From the same **Information** panel you can also check whether an image contains one or more bands by looking at the **Dimensions** field.

[2]QGIS: qgis.org

Processing

To begin processing a multispectral dataset with WebODM, select all images from all bands when creating a new task.

The multispectral processing pipeline is similar to a normal dataset pipeline. First, a band is automatically selected as the primary band. Then all images belonging to that band are used for the SFM/MVS steps. Note that because of this, the point cloud and textured model will take on the colors of the primary band only.

The selection of the primary band is automatically determined by the value of the XMP tags in the images (**DLS:SensorId** and **Camera:RigCameraIndex**). The images with the lowest value are selected as the primary band. If the tag is missing, a band is selected based on the order in which images are read from disk, which is an undefined behavior (but will still work in most cases). One can manually specify the primary band with the primary-band option, which takes the name of the band that you want to use as primary. The name must match the value specified in the **Camera:BandName** XMP tag (we cover examining EXIF/XMP tags in The Command Line chapter). It might be useful to manually specify a primary band in cases where the reconstruction on the default band fails.

Once reconstruction of the primary band has completed, the images from the remaining bands are aligned to the primary band. This alignment can compensate for small imaging differences due to the positional offsets of the band sensors, but is unable to compensate for more complex shifts. In short, ODX will not be able to properly align band images that have been captured with different lenses or with sensors mounted far apart.

Red, green and blue multispectral images of the same area

Combining the original images shows misalignment (left) and the same images after alignment (right)

After all images have been aligned, 3D models are generated for each band and an orthophoto is created by taking pictures from above of each one. The final result is combined into a single GeoTIFF. Internally the band order of the resulting GeoTIFF is determined by the **DLS:SensorId** and **Camera:RigCameraIndex** XMP tags, so remember that the first band might not necessarily be what you'd expect. In the case of RGB images, Red is not always the first band. You can check the results with QGIS[3]. From the layers list right-click the orthophoto and select **Properties... — Information** and scroll

[3]QGIS: qgis.org

down to the **Bands** section.

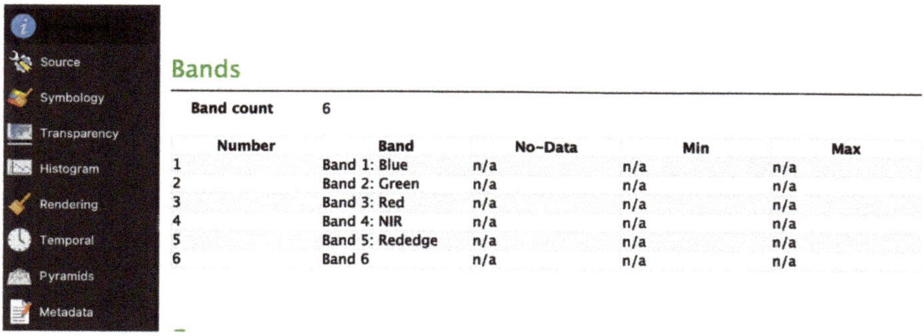

Orthophoto band information in QGIS

WebODM will automatically choose the proper RGB band order when showing the orthophoto from **Map** view.

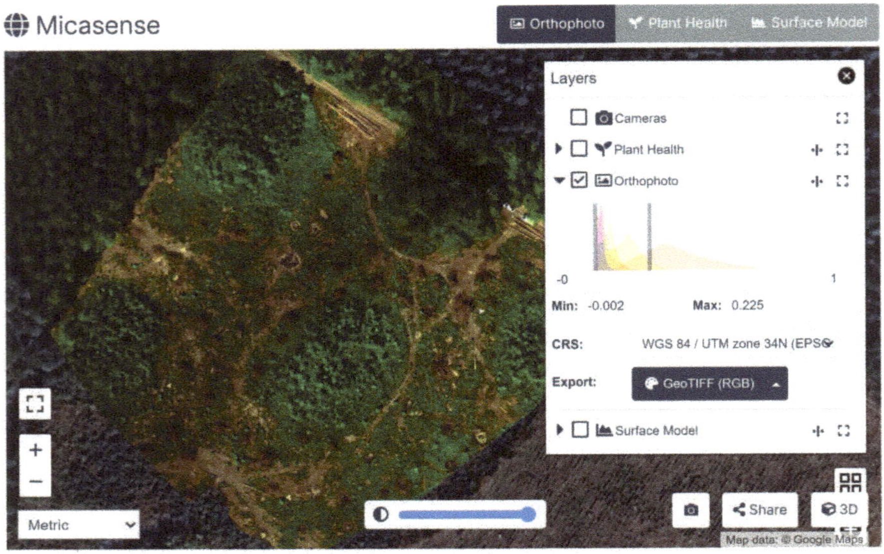

In this dataset the orthophoto's internal band order is BGR, but WebODM displays it correctly as RGB

Looking at the screenshot above you might have noticed that the minimum and maximum values displayed in the layer list are between 0 and 1 instead of the usual 0-255 (or 0-65535). That's because the dataset was processed with the radiometric calibration option.

Radiometric Calibration Basics

The end goal of radiometric calibration is to obtain useful information about stuff on the ground (e.g. crops) so that we can perform measurements. Pixel values (digital numbers) are just a measure of light intensity. But the light intensity values have been influenced by factors we don't care about. When we take pictures from the sky, there are things that get in the way. The unique characteristics of the sensor, the air in the atmosphere, the intensity and angle of the sun. Finally, the stuff on the ground affects those values. These factors all add up to form the pixel values of an image.

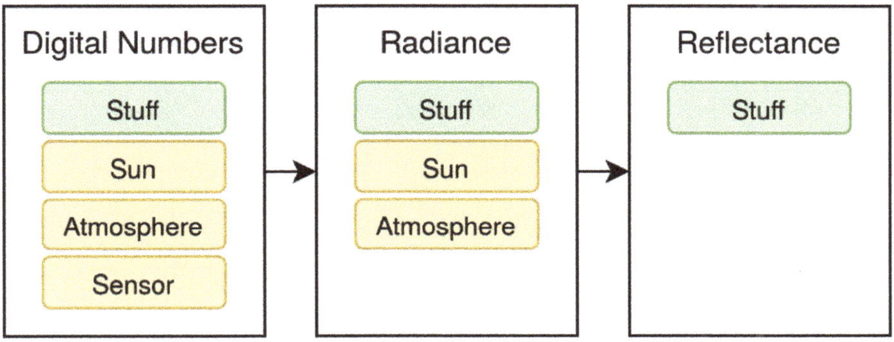

Radiometric calibration is the process during which unwanted factors from pixel values are removed to obtain reflectance values (measureable information about stuff on the ground)

Reflectance is a value between 0 and 1 and indicates how much light is reflected by stuff on the ground compared to the amount of light that falls onto it. For example, a value of 0 indicates that no light is reflected and the stuff on the ground is absorbing all light. A value of 1 indicates that all light is reflected.

ODX can perform basic radiometric calibration automatically using two modes of operation, **camera** and **camera+sun**. These can be enabled via the radiometric-calibration option:

Option	Description
camera	Applies sensor corrections. These include black level, vignetting, gain and exposure corrections.
camera+sun	Applies all the corrections of **camera**, plus sun and atmosphere corrections using a downwelling light sensor (DLS) if available.

The atmosphere correction makes the assumption that photos are captured on a day with clear skies. If that is not the case, the values might not be accurate.

Regardless of the choice of radiometric calibration method, if high accuracy is required, the use of calibrated reflectance panels is a must. These panels are specially designed surfaces or objects with known and precisely measured reflectance properties. They are used as a reference for calibrating measurements of light reflectance. At the time of writing, ODX does not support automated reflectance panel calibration. In this case, images should be first calibrated with the sensor's manufacturer's software and processed in ODX afterwards.

If the images have already been corrected for alignment outside of ODX, it's recommended to use the skip-band-alignment option.

Keep in mind that unless the texturing-skip-global-seam-leveling option is used, radiance values will be altered to achieve a seamless orthophoto. Turn on this option if you're using calibration panels and want to preserve reflectance values.

Viewing Results in WebODM

WebODM offers a convenient **Plant Health** tab under **Map** view for viewing multispectral orthophotos.

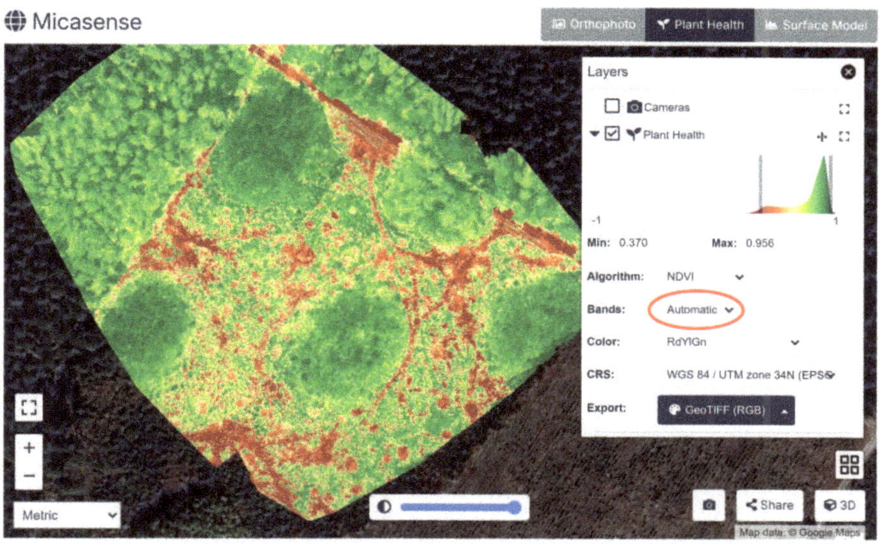

Plant Health tab

While using the Plant Health tab, WebODM will attempt to automatically detect the order of the bands of the orthophoto. If that's not possible, a small warning icon will be displayed next to the **Bands** field from the **Layers** panel. In that case, it's important to select the correct value manually. Let's look at a few examples:

Bands	Band 1	Band 2	Band 3	Band 4	Band 5
RGN	Red	Green	Near-infrared	Ignore	Ignore
BGRNRe	Blue	Green	Red	Near-infrared	Red-edge

If the map does not seem to display correctly (does it look like a single colored blob?), adjust the **Min** and **Max** ranges.

It's possible to select a variety of algorithms for analysis. Hovering the cursor over the name of an algorithm for a few seconds brings up a tooltip with a description of the algorithm and the underlying formula used to compute it. What do these algorithms do? They help to highlight different characteristics of the reflectance values and each algorithm typically is useful to achieve a certain analysis goal.

For example, the Normalized Difference Vegetation Index (NDVI) is used to quantify health and density of vegetation cover. It is defined by:

```
NDVI = (NIR - Red) / (NIR + Red)
```

It's a number between -1 and +1, with values closer to +1 indicating healthier vegetation and values closer to -1 indicating less healthy or non-vegetation areas.

It's outside of the scope of this book to cover all available algorithms, but descriptions are only a quick internet search away.

Thermal Datasets

Long-wave Infrared (LWIR) sensors are able to capture radiant heat (temperature) information. Processing LWIR images works the same way as processing multispectral images, but with LWIR images radiometric calibration converts pixel values to temperature values (in degrees Celsius) instead of reflectance values. To get temperature values, enable the radiometric-calibration option, unless you have a DJI drone (more information below). If you don't get good values, check if your sensor is actually supported[4].

For best results, LWIR images should be at least 640x480 pixels and captured with 90% overlap/sidelap. It's sometimes possible to process LWIR images as small as 240x180 pixels if they are processed as part of a multispectral dataset, with the primary band being one with bigger images. Processing smaller images might fail or result in alignment issues.

[4]Supported Thermal Hardware: docs.webodm.org/multispectral/#hardware

Temperature can be viewed from WebODM under the **Thermal** tab and selecting the **Celsius** algorithm

Most newer DJI drones require thermal images to be pre-processed with Thermal Tools[5], a free application built for WebODM that calibrates the images before processing. After pre-processing with Thermal Tools, upload the converted images and make sure the radiometric-calibration is disabled, as the images will be already calibrated.

[5]Thermal Tools: github.com/uav4geo/Thermal-Tools

10. Image Masks

Image masking is a feature that allows users to specify which parts of an image should be left out during reconstruction. This can be useful for removing noise or unwanted items.

Input image (left) and image mask for the same image removing the sky (right). Black areas are ignored during reconstruction

Image mask images must have the same pixel dimensions as the image they are masking and must be named **[filename]_mask.png** or **[filename]_mask.jpg**. For example, the image mask for **IMG_0001.JPG** should be named **IMG_0001_mask.png** or **IMG_0001_mask.jpg**.

Note that to remove an unwanted item from the results it's necessary to mask the item in *every* image where the item appears. Masking the item in a single image is not sufficient if the item is also present in other images.

Image masks can be automatically generated using the sky-removal and bg-removal options, or they can be created manually. When these options are used, image masks are created using an AI model that has been trained to recognize background items or the sky. Masks are created during the dataset stage of the processing pipeline.

Manually Creating Image Masks

While automatic generation of image masks is certainly more efficient, it doesn't cover all cases and sometimes masks need to be created manually. There are multiple ways to create image masks with your favorite image editor. Below you can find a procedure on how to do it with the free and open source GIMP[1]. Photopea[2] is also a free alternative to consider where the workflow is similar.

Step 1. Open the Target Image

After you've installed GIMP, drag & drop the target image into it or open it via **File — Open**.

[1]GIMP: gimp.org

[2]Photopea Online Photo Editor: photopea.com

Look for the **Layers** panel and find the **Create New Layer** button. Alternatively you can also open the **Layer** menu and select **New Layer...**.

Step 2. Create a New Layer

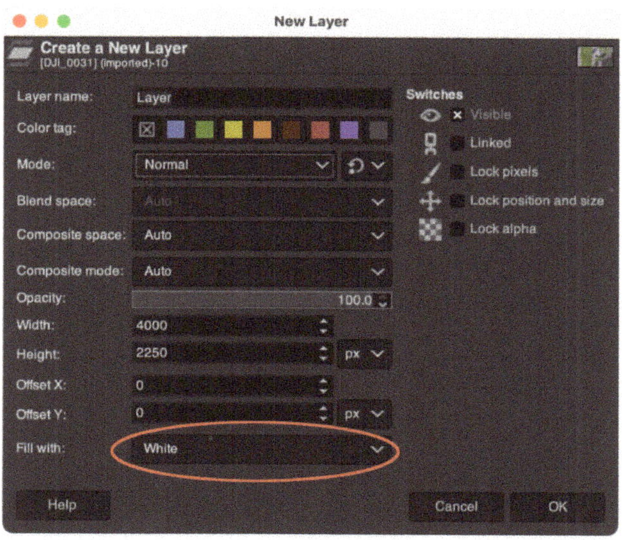

Make sure to select **White** from the **Fill with** field.

Step 3. Paint the Mask

- With the new layer selected, slide the **Opacity** slider to **30%**.
- Select the **Paintbrush Tool**.
- Set the foreground/background colors to pure black and pure white. You can go to **Tools — Default Colors** to do that.
- Select the **Pixel** brush and adjust the **Size**.
- Start painting the items you want to remove using the black color.

Masking a building

Step 4. Export the Mask

- Slide the **Opacity** slider back to **100%**.
- Go to **File — Export As...** and save the image mask by adding the **_mask** suffix to the original filename.

Repeat for every other image that contains the item.

11. Rolling Shutter Correction

Many consumer-grade cameras use an imaging method known as a "rolling shutter". Instead of instantaneously capturing the entire image, like "global shutter" cameras do, rolling shutter cameras capture an image by quickly scanning a picture line-by-line (or column-by-column). This scanning does not happen instantaneously, instead it's performed over a fraction of a second. This is not an issue if the camera is stationary, but if the camera is moving a rolling shutter distortion effect will be present in the final image.

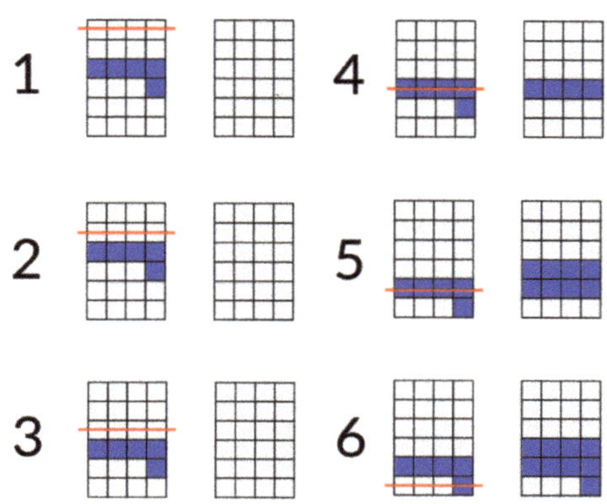

Rolling shutter effect: what the sensor sees (left columns) vs. how the final image is stored (right columns) at different time intervals (1-6)

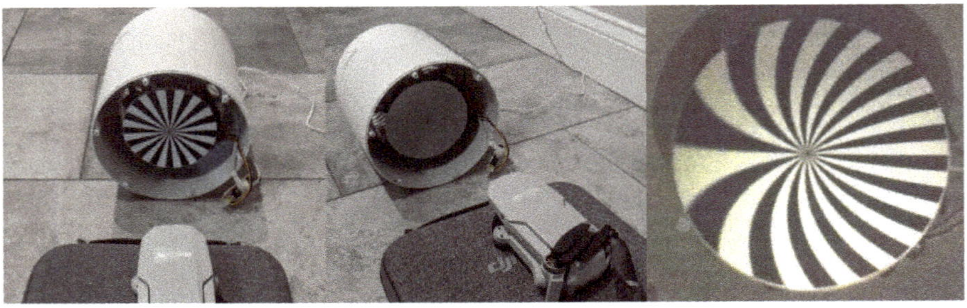

Rolling shutter effect. Stationary calibration pattern (left), moving calibration pattern (center) and image captured with rolling shutter camera (right). Notice the distortion

An animation showing the rolling shutter effect is also available on Wikipedia[1].

Usage

Rolling shutter correction can be enabled by using the rolling-shutter option.

If GPS information is available from the input images and the dataset was captured with a single camera, ODX can compensate for rolling shutter distortion by first estimating the velocity of the aircraft at any time that a picture was taken. Some cameras store velocity information in the EXIF/XMP tags of the images (**SpeedX**, **SpeedY** and **SpeedZ**). This is the most reliable estimate. If no tags are available, the velocity is estimated based on the time and positional difference between consecutive images:

```
speed = (position_2 - position_1) / (time_2 - time_1)
```

[1]Rolling shutter: en.wikipedia.org/wiki/Rolling_shutter

This is not always correct, as the assumption in the formula above is that the drone is always moving and that images are captured sequentially. For example, if the drone is stationary while capturing a picture, the calculation will yield an incorrect estimate and will probably make results worse. As long as most images can be assigned good velocity estimates, rolling shutter correction can perform its job, even if a few images have incorrect estimates.

After velocities have been estimated, the program searches a database to find the rolling shutter readout time for the camera sensor. This is the time (in milliseconds) that it takes for the sensor to capture an image. If your camera is not available in the database, you will find a warning in the task output that reads:

```
[WARNING] Rolling shutter readout time for "make model" is
not in our database, using default of 30ms which might be
incorrect.
```

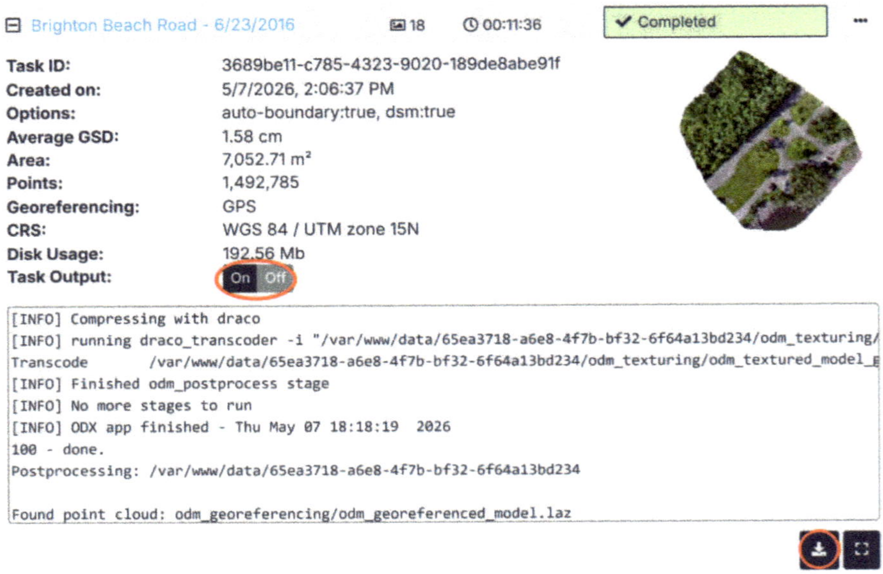

You can access the task output by expanding a task from the **Dashboard** and toggling the **Task Output** button to **On**. If the task output is truncated, first you'll need to download the task output to a file by pressing the **Download To File** button

You can manually specify the correct sensor readout time by using the rolling-shutter-readout option. The correct value for your sensor can be estimated by building an inexpensive calibration device with an Arduino by following the instructions published on github.com/WebODM/RSCalibration.

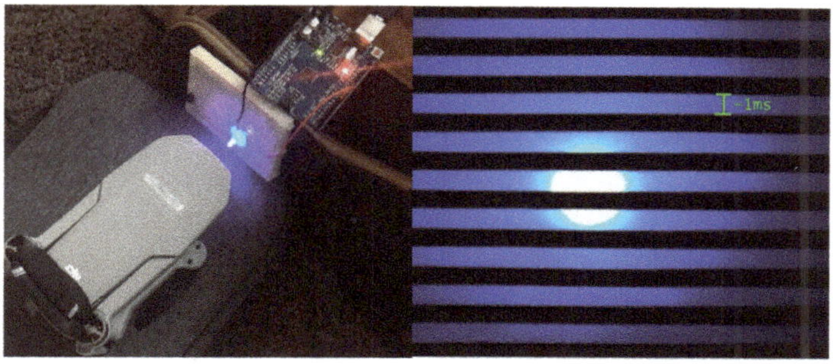

Finding out your sensor's readout time is a fun weekend project and an excellent way to contribute back to WebODM by contributing your sensor's value to our database

With known camera velocities and sensor readout time at hand, the correction is performed by applying a shift (computed from these two factors) to the image features. The SFM step is then repeated for a second time. This increases the processing time, but helps increase accuracy in datasets affected by rolling shutter distortions.

Limitations

Rolling shutter correction can help improve the accuracy of a dataset captured in motion with a rolling shutter sensor. However, if high accuracy is required, it should not be used as a substitute for good data capture practices or for avoiding the purchase of better hardware. Instructing the mission planning software to stop-and-hover while taking pictures will drastically reduce the effect of rolling shutter in rolling shutter cameras. A global shutter camera is always preferable with software like ODX and will yield more accurate results.

12. Camera Calibration

In order to create accurate reconstructions, the software needs to know the internal details of the cameras used for taking the photos. These details are referred to as *intrinsic camera parameters* and include values such as focal lengths, camera centers and distortion parameters. Reading the specification values from the manufacturer or looking this information from a database is not sufficient to get accurate values. Defects in the manufacturing process, vibrations and other factors can cause these values to vary, even between identical camera models.

You might have noticed that you can process datasets and obtain good results without performing any kind of camera calibration. This is because modern photogrammetry software (including ODX) performs a kind of self-calibration directly from the input images. Self-calibration tends to work very well in ODX, as long as:

1. Images are captured at different elevations.
2. Images are captured at varying angles (including both nadir and angled shots).

High overlap, near nadir images are not recommended[1]. This is important to remember, as most mission planning software will create exactly this type of pattern.

[1]Camera Calibration Considerations for UAV Photogrammetry: https://www.isprs.org/tc2-symposium2018/images/ISPRS-Invited-Fraser.pdf

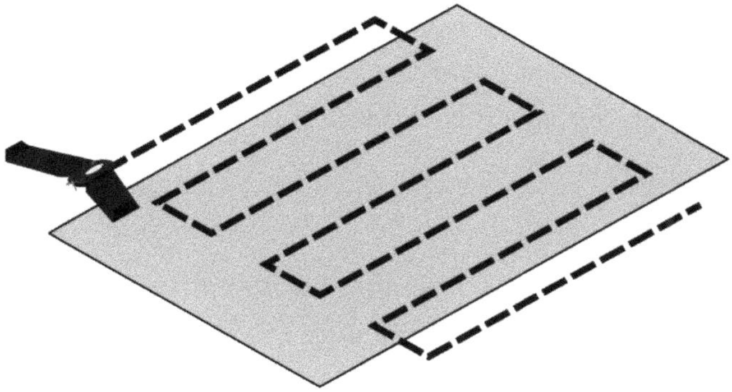

Typical flight path from mission planning software. Not great for self-calibration

This doesn't mean a person should never fly this pattern. It just means that when flying this pattern, people need to be aware that the internal camera parameters' estimates will not be as good. Inaccurate parameters lead to an improper camera lens model, which over large areas typically results in a *doming* effect.

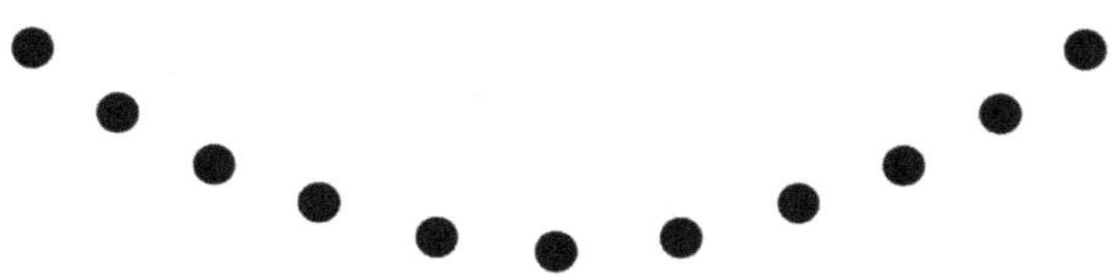

Point cloud exhibiting doming. The terrain appears arched instead of straight

Doming is best cured by following best practices while collecting aerial imagery: flying at different elevations (maximize scale variation) and varying angles.

Unfortunately the luxury of capturing perfect images is not always available. Perhaps a dataset has already been captured and there's no opportunity for a retake, or the area is too large to cover in multiple passes.

To attempt to correct this problem, it's possible to use an existing camera model obtained from a good dataset (lots of overlap, varying elevations, different angles, etc.) captured with the same camera and reuse the camera parameters obtained from self-calibration on a different dataset.

With WebODM

After processing a good dataset, click **Download - Camera Parameters**.

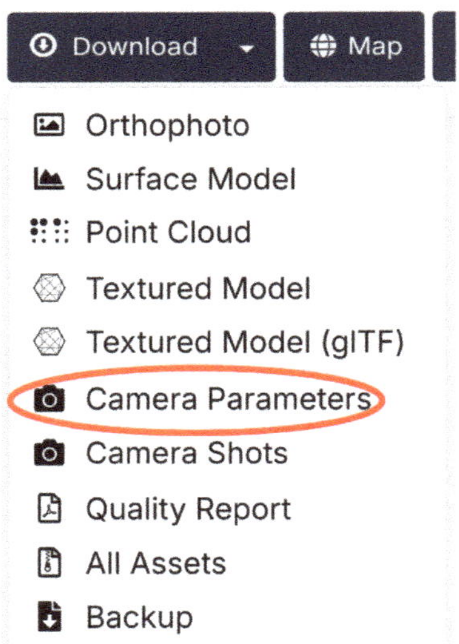

This will save a **cameras.json** file. When creating a new task, from the task options set the **cameras** option by selecting the **cameras.json** file. The dataset will be processed using the camera parameters previously computed.

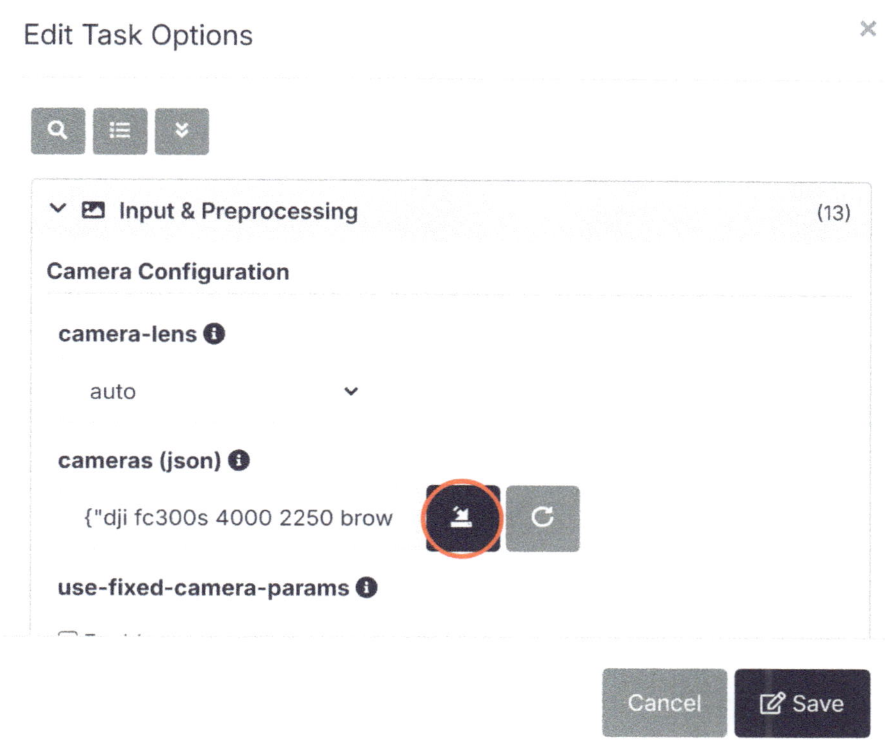

Click the cameras button to import a cameras.json file to use for camera calibration

With ODX

After processing is complete, a **cameras.json** file is always saved in the root directory of the project. To reuse camera parameters from an existing project, pass a path to a **cameras.json** file via the cameras option.

For example, if **cameras.json** is stored in **D:\book\projects\first**:

```
(odx) C:\ODX> run d:\book\projects\second --cameras
↪ d:\book\projects\first\cameras.json
```

Command line usage is covered in more details in The Command Line chapter.

13. Report Analysis

After a dataset has been processed, it's important to understand if the results are good or not. The PDF report provides a good starting point for this type of analysis.

In WebODM, after a dataset has finished processing, the PDF report is available by expanding a task from the **Dashboard** and selecting **Download — Quality Report**, or by pressing the **Report** button.

While reading this chapter, I encourage readers to follow along with a copy of a PDF report generated by the software. It will provide more context to the descriptions.

Note that some fields might not be displayed if a dataset lacks georeferencing.

Dataset Summary

Field	Description
Date	Date and time the dataset was processed
Area Coverage	Calculated using a box drawn around all camera positions. This is not the area of the orthophoto
Processing Time	Time it took to process the dataset

Field	Description
Capture Start	Time of the first photo in the dataset as indicated in the EXIF tags
Capture End	Time of the last photo in the dataset as indicated in the EXIF tags
Coordinate Reference System	Coordinate reference system of the outputs

Processing Summary

Field Description	
Reconstructed Images	Number of images used to compute the results
Reconstructed Points (Sparse)	Number of points extracted during the SFM step
Reconstructed Points (Dense)	Number of points in the output point cloud
Average Ground Sampling Distance (GSD)	Real average distance represented by two adjacent pixels in the input images
Detected Features	Number of image features detected during SFM
Reconstructed Features	Number of image features used for reconstruction during SFM
Geographic Reference	**GPS**: GPS was used for georeferencing

Field	Description
	GCP: GCPs were used for georeferencing **GPS and GCP**: Both GPS and GCPs were used for georeferencing **Alignment**: The dataset was aligned to another via the align option **None**: Dataset was not georeferenced
GPS/GCP/Alignment Errors	The absolute average error of the geographic reference

The image that follows shows the trajectory of the cameras and a preview of the sparse point cloud computed during SFM. This image is not aligned geographically so it's normal for it to appear in a different orientation that the other outputs.

Previews

If an orthophoto or DEMs are available, they are displayed in this section.

Survey Data

This section begins with a picture of the point cloud rendered with colors that indicate the number of photos that were used to generate a certain section. It's important to note that this image is different and more useful than a simple image overlap diagram. It can highlight areas that might have had sufficient overlap coverage, but insufficient details for the SFM process to reconstruct points using all images.

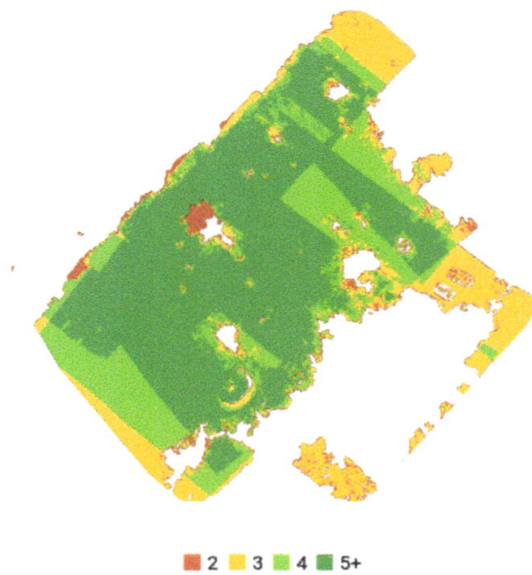

For best results, aim to have as much dark green (5+) coverage as possible

The number of cameras used to reconstruct each individual point is also stored in the **odm_georeferenced_model.laz** point cloud in the **UserData** dimension.

GPS/GCP/3D Errors Details

Errors are differences between values that are measured vs. the values that are computed. When estimating GPS and GCP errors, the program has at its disposal measurements of real world locations acquired with a GPS device. After processing has completed, those same locations in the model will deviate slightly from the real world measurements, due to factors such as inaccuracy of the GPS device, camera lens distortion and computational inaccuracies during the reconstruction process.

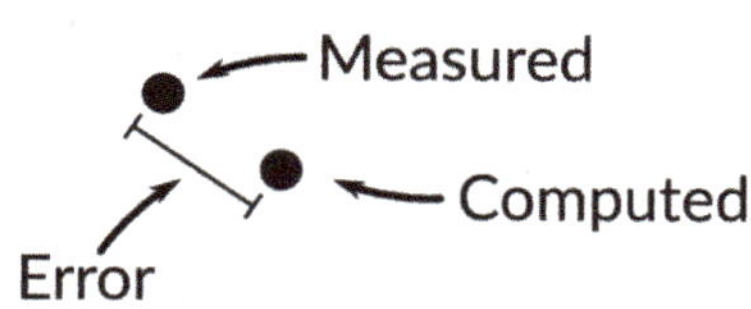

Error is the difference between measured and computed values

3D errors give us information about the relative accuracy of the reconstruction. For example, if an object in the real world is 1 meter long, but the reconstructed model ends up being 1.05 meters long, the 3D error can be calculated as:

```
import math
actual = 1
measured = 1.05
print(math.sqrt((actual - measured)**2)) # <-- 0.05
```

Since 3D errors do not have real world measurements to compare against. To compute it, each point from the sparse point cloud is visualized (back-projected) from the point of view of the cameras that generated it. Since each point in 3D has its genesis traced back to points from multiple 2D images (image feature locations), it's possible to first estimate a pixel reprojection error:

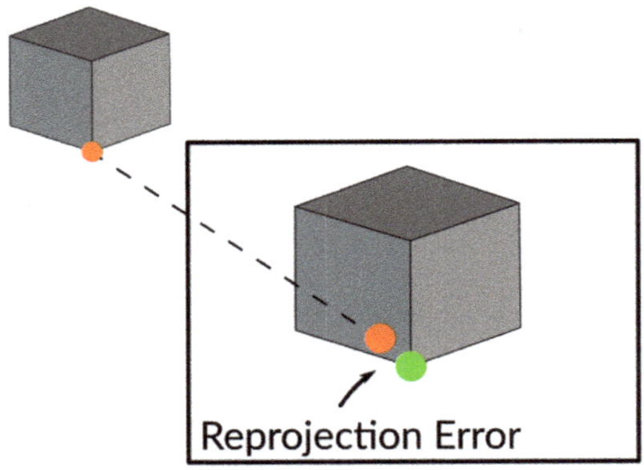

Since the reprojection error is in pixels, but we're interested in real world units (meters), the program iteratively triangulates 3D points by sampling points around the reprojection area, trying to find the combination of points that gives the maximum 3D error.

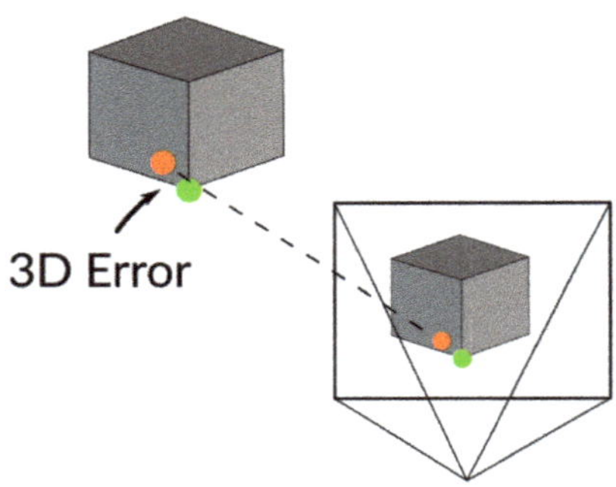

One triangulation iteration for computing a 3D error. Simplified by showing a single camera. Multiple iterations and multiple cameras are involved during the search for the maximum 3D error for a single 3D point

If this sounds a bit confusing, don't worry! The key point to remember is that 3D errors are a measure of relative accuracy.

The values that are displayed in the report's tables are calculated from several error measurements and condensed into single metrics. In the case of GPS, there's one measurement for each image that has GPS information. For GCPs, there's one measurement for each GCP entry. For 3D there's 1000 measurements sampled from the sparse point cloud.

When we're talking about error, since we're referring to 3D measures, we always break it down into its X, Y (horizontal) and Z (vertical) components. Each component has three metrics:

Metric	Description
Mean	The average error across all measurements
Standard Deviation	A measure of how spread out the measurements are from the average value
RMS Error	The Root Mean Square error, which is an averaging metric that ignores whether errors are positive or negative

```
import math
errors = [0.1, 0.2, 0.3]

mean = sum(errors) / len(errors)
std_dev = math.sqrt(sum([((e - mean) ** 2) for e in errors]) /
↪  len(errors))
rms = math.sqrt(sum([e ** 2 for e in errors]) / len(errors))
print(mean, std_dev, rms) # <-- 0.2, 0.0816, 0.216
```

The **Total** is a metric representing the overall average error in the X/Y/Z dimensions. It's computed by:

```
x_errors = (0.1, 0.2, 0.3, 0.4)
y_errors = (0.3, 0.4, 0.5, 0.6)
z_errors = (0.1, 0.2, 0.3, 0.4)

errors = [math.sqrt(x_errors[i] ** 2 +
                    y_errors[i] ** 2 +
                    z_errors[i] ** 2)
            for i in range(4)]

total = sum(errors) / len(errors)
print(total) # <-- 0.575
```

An intuitive way to think of the computation above is that we're adding together the X/Y/Z components for each error measurement and averaging the results to get a total.

Another useful set of metrics computed around the error measurements are the relative and absolute accuracy measures. Absolute accuracy is computed from GCP error measurements, with GPS as a fallback if no GCPs are available. It measures the accuracy of the reconstruction in relation to its real position in the world. Relative accuracy is computed from 3D error measurements and relates the accuracy of the reconstruction to its expected real dimensions.

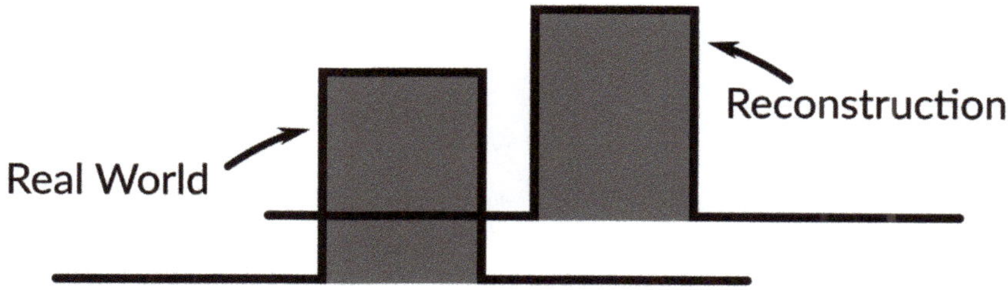

This building was reconstructed with high relative accuracy but low absolute accuracy

The report provides Circular Error (CE90) and Linear Error (LE90) estimates for horizontal (X/Y) and vertical (Z) errors respectively. The number 90 means that the software is 90% confident that the reported value is equal or better than the actual value[1].

It's important to be careful while interpreting these accuracy numbers, especially in the absence of ground control points. The uncertainty from GPS measurements is not modeled into these values, and the estimates will only be as good as the precision of your GPS device. Always verify the accuracy of a reconstruction with checkpoints by measuring points on the ground.

Feature Details

This section has information about the image features extracted during the SFM step.

[1] Computation of scalar accuracy metrics LE, CE, and SE as both predictive and sample based statistics: masseranolabs.com/IGTF2016-000255.pdf

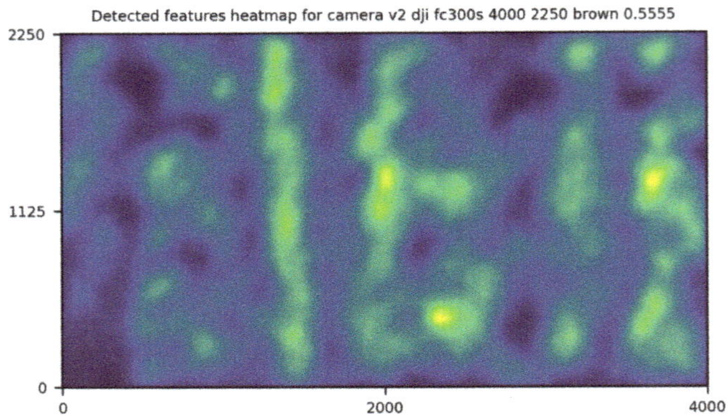

The features heatmap highlights the distribution of feature locations across a single camera. Yellow areas indicate more features

For best camera calibration results, the heatmap should look smooth, with few or no patches of dark purple.

The table that follows lists the minimum, maximum, average (mean) and most common (median) number of detected and reconstructed features for each image. Reconstructed features are features that have been used for triangulating points. The **Reconstructed Min.** field is particularly interesting and should be above 50. A value less than 50 indicates that one or more images didn't have many good quality features. Increasing the min-num-features option will affect these values.

Reconstruction Details

Average Reprojection Error

Earlier in the chapter we introduced the concept of reprojection error (measured in pixels) when talking about 3D errors. The reprojection error can also be calculated in normalized coordinates (unit-less) or as an angle (in radians). Average values computed across all features are reported in this section.

Unit	Description
Normalized	Every image feature has a *scale* parameter that describes how many pixels the feature spans. Normalized values are obtained by dividing the reprojection error (in pixels) of a feature by its scale
Pixels	Reprojection error (in pixels)
Angular	The angle (in radians) between the original feature and its projection

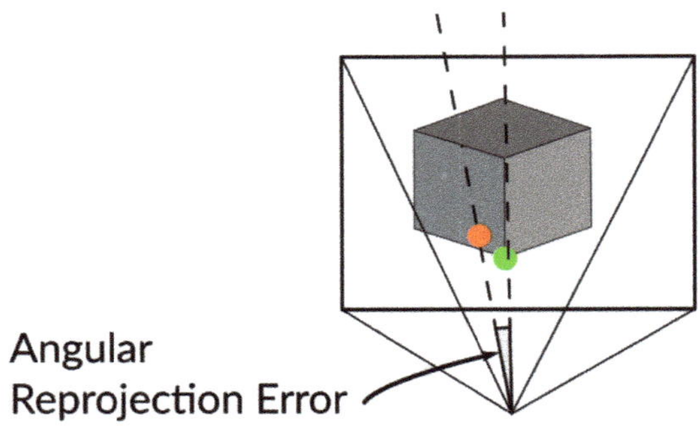

Visualizing two rays passing through the camera center to find the angular reprojection error

To convert from radians to degrees one can use:

```
import math
angle = 1.5707
print(math.degrees(angle)) # <-- ~90
```

Doesn't matter what your favorite unit is. The important part to understand is that smaller reprojection errors = better.

Average Track Length

A track is a set of corresponding image features identified on multiple images that depict the same object.

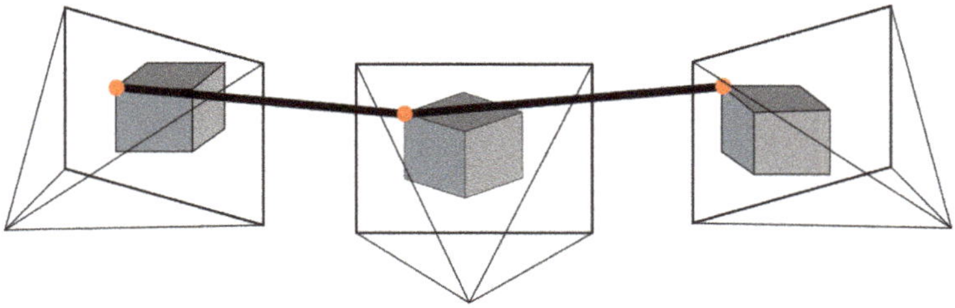

A track of length 3

This number is the average number of images that have been used to reconstruct a point.

Average Track Length (> 2)

Same as above, but without taking into consideration tracks of length 2, which are considered to be of low quality.

This number is the average number of images that have been used to reconstruct a point when at least three images were used.

When it comes to track length, the higher the better.

Normalized/Pixel/Angular Residuals

These graphs show the distribution of the reprojection errors across all points. On the horizontal axis you have the reprojection error, on the vertical axis you have the number of points that have that reprojection error. “Residual” in this context is used to refer to the reprojection error.

Track Details

The graph in this section shows the connectivity between image matches. The nodes represent images and the connections represent a match between two images. Each connection is colored according to the number of common image features that were successfully matched between images. An ideal graph shows a large number of connections.

The table that follows lists the distribution of points vs. the number of images that were used to generate those points (track length).

Row	Description
Length	The number of images
Count	How many points were generated from **Length** images

An ideal dataset should have most points generated from 3 or more images.

Camera Models Details

This section starts by showing information about the cameras' internal parameters.

The table lists the parameters of the cameras' lens model before (**Initial**) and after optimization (**Optimized**). Normally the optimized parameters will deviate from the initial values, but not by much. A very large difference between initial and optimized parameters can represent possible issues, such as the choice of a wrong camera-lens model.

The camera residuals grid displays information about the distribution of the average reprojection errors (residuals) across all images for a particular camera.

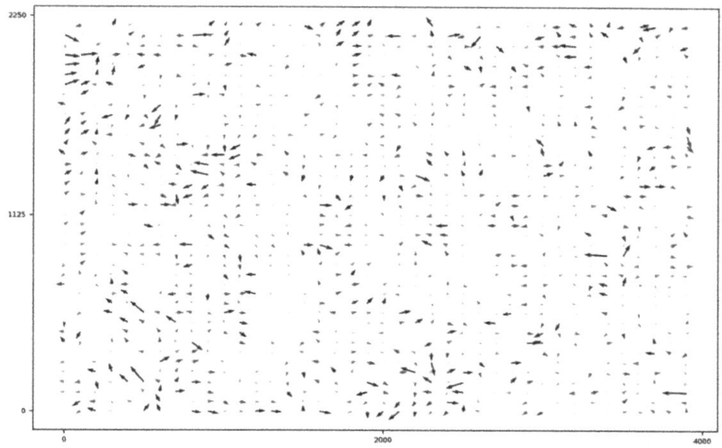

Some large reprojection errors are exhibited in this grid

This is the same reprojection error information that we've covered earlier in this chapter, but this time it's displayed as arrows on an image plane. Each arrow represents the size (and direction) of the average reprojection error for each image feature at that location. In other words: long and dark purple arrows represent *large* average reprojection errors at that particular location. Short and orange-colored arrows represent *small* average reprojection errors. The horizontal axis of the grid is the image width, the vertical axis is the image height.

The **Residual Norm** bar shows the color scale of the normalized reprojection errors. If the maximum value on this bar is 0.16, it means that a dark purple arrow in the grid indicates a reprojection error of 0.16 (in scaled, normalized units). The difference between the maximum value and the minimum value of the bar is the **Residual grid scale** value.

An ideal dataset should have a low **Residual grid scale** and small arrows throughout the image plane.

JSON output

The information in the PDF report is great for humans to read, but what about machines?

The same information from the PDF report (minus the graphics) is also available as a JSON[2] file in **odm_report/stats.json**. From WebODM you can find it by going to **Download — All Assets** and extracting the resulting archive.

[2]JavaScript Object Notation (JSON): json.org

14. Flying Tips

Data collection is sometimes more art than science. There are however many useful guidelines you can follow to increase the quality and accuracy of your results. Follow these recommendations and you will achieve better results.

Fly Higher

This is probably the most useful tip. Once you know the target resolution you're aiming for, don't fly lower than you absolutely need. If you need an orthophoto at 5 cm / pixel resolution, don't fly at an altitude that gives you a 1 cm / pixel resolution. Most flight planner apps will tell you what altitude you need to fly to achieve a target resolution. This is not only for saving space and processing time: the results will look better also! When you fly at a higher elevation more features can be matched across images during the structure from motion process (especially for areas with lots of trees or vegetation). Building rooftops will also look better due to the fact that higher altitude reduces the amount of distortion near building edges. Finally, you can achieve greater image overlap and cover a larger area in a single flight.

Fly on Overcast Days

When possible, try to plan your flights when clouds are covering the sky. Clouds diffuse the rays from the sun, creating a soft light that reduces blur, shadows and produces more pleasing colors, increasing the overall quality of orthophotos and 3D models.

Fly Between 10am and 2pm

When the sun is directly above you, there will be less shadows and more uniform lighting.

Fly at Different Elevations and Capture Multiple Angles

ODX can produce more accurate results when you capture images from different elevations, using both nadir (straight down) and non-nadir (at an angle) images. A cross pattern flown at two different altitudes with varying angles is much better than a single nadir-only pattern. When capturing angled images, be careful to set a value that avoids the horizon! Capturing the horizon can deteriorate results instead of improving them.

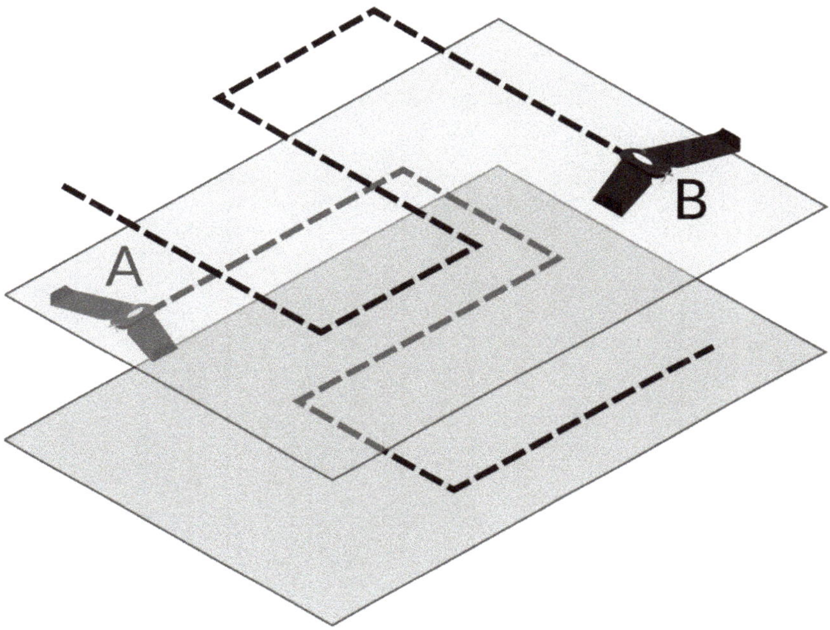

Flying cross-pattern at different elevations with B capturing nadir images and A capturing images at a slight angle (or vice-versa) is a better for camera calibration

We discuss this in more details in the Camera Calibration chapter.

Fly on Calm Days

When it's windy your drone will have a harder time stabilizing the camera and can produce images that are blurrier. Fly when it's calm for better results.

Increase Overlap

More overlap increases the number of features that can be matched across images. Side overlap is more important than front overlap, so increase side overlap first, then increase front overlap.

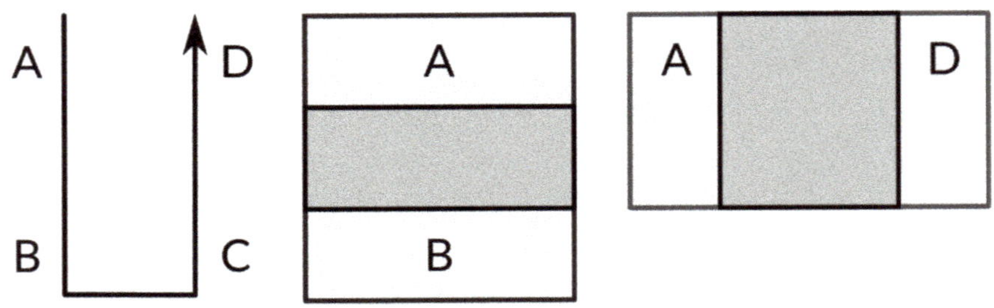

Flight path with 4 images (left), front overlap (middle) and side overlap (right). Darker areas indicate the overlap area between images. More overlap is better

Set Drone to Hover While Taking Images

If your drone camera is equipped with a rolling shutter camera (most consumer grade drones), you should instruct the flight controller to bring the drone to a hover before taking a picture. Doing this will increase the accuracy of the reconstruction. This is not something to worry about if your drone camera is equipped with a global shutter. If you cannot avoid taking the images in motion while using a rolling shutter camera, make sure to enable the rolling-shutter option for processing.

Check Camera Settings

Make sure that image quality is set to high and auto focus is disabled. To do that, fly at your target altitude before mission start, set the focus, then disable auto focus.

This chapter concludes the first part of the book. Most of what you need to know to start using WebODM efficiently has been covered. Congratulations for making it this far!

The second part delves into some more advanced topics, such as using ODX from the command line, the mysteries of docker, leveraging the GPU, processing humongous datasets at scale and an introduction to using Python for automating processing using the NodeODX API.

Part III.

Advanced Usages

15. The Command Line

In the first part of this book we explored how to use WebODM, the friendly graphical interface to ODX. WebODM hides some of the complexities of ODX, but this convenience comes at a cost. Here are a few things you cannot easily do in WebODM:

- Process tasks without first copying/uploading them to WebODM
- Inspect intermediate result files
- Restart a task from an arbitrary point in the pipeline (WebODM supports task restarts, but only for a subset of them)
- Restart tasks without time expirations (WebODM can restart tasks only within 2 days of the task completing, unless the NodeODX settings are changed)

In this chapter we're going to leave the comforts of the user interface and dive into the realm of power users, using the command line to process the tasks directly with ODX.

This is not meant to be an exhaustive guide on using the command line for different operating systems. It's an overview of the basic commands you'll likely need to know for the purpose of using ODX.

If you are already familiar with the command line, feel free to skip this chapter.

Installation

If you're on Windows and you have installed WebODM with the Windows Installer, you'll find the **ODX Console** application (console.bat) in a subfolder at **C:\WebODM\resources\app\apps\ODX** (your drive / path might be slightly different). If you need to install ODX on a new machine, download the latest Windows setup from github.com/WebODM/ODX/releases.

On Linux and macOS simply make sure that docker is installed as described in the Getting Started chapter or by visiting docker.com.

Command Line Basics

First, we should clarify that a *command line* is any application that allows a user to interact with it by means of typing commands. There are many varieties of command line applications and each operating system tends to have its own flavors. To provide a unified set of instructions for all three major operating systems (Windows, macOS, Linux), when we say *command line* we will always refer to *Bash* or one of its variants:

- Windows: use the **ODX Console** (installation instructions below). Do **not** use the Command Prompt or Powershell
- macOS: use the **Terminal** app
- Linux: Most distributions already use **Bash** by default, but in case your shell is different, just launch a bash shell by typing **bash** in your terminal

Below are some commands you should be familiar with. Once you have opened a command line, try to type them:

Windows:

- **dir:** list files and directories
- **cd <dir>**: change directory (same as Linux/Mac)
- **cd:** show me the current directory (cd without arguments)
- **<N>:** switch to drive N (e.g. `D:` switches to the D drive)
- **type <file>**: show the contents of file
- **more <file>:** show the contents of file page by page
- **dir /s *.JPG:** find all JPG files in the current directory (and subdirectories)
- **whoami:** show the name of the current user

macOS/Linux:

- **ls -al:** list files and directories
- **cd <dir>**: change directory
- **pwd**: show me the current directory
- **cat <file>**: show the contents of file
- **head -n <lines> <file>:** show the first lines of file
- **tail -n <lines> <file>:** show the last lines of file
- **find . -name *.JPG:** find all JPG files in the current directory (and subdirectories)
- **whoami:** show the name of the current user
- **chown -R $(whoami):$(whoami) <directory>**: change ownership of directory to the current user and group
- **sudo <command>**: execute command with admin privileges

Adding a `/?` (Windows) or `--help` (macOS/Linux) flag to any of the commands above will show a description of the command along with usage information.

```
$ ls --help
Usage: ls [OPTION]... [FILE]...
```

```
List information about the FILEs (the current directory by
 ↪  default).
Sort entries alphabetically if none of -cftuvSUX nor --sort is
 ↪  specified.
```

Paths on macOS and Linux are separated by forward slashes (as in **/c/Users/myuser**). This is sometimes a source of confusion for Windows users who are used to back slashes (as in **C:\Users\myuser**). Paths and filenames are also case-sensitive, so **/c/file** is different than **/c/FiLe**. On Windows paths are not case-sensitive.

Pressing the **TAB** key while typing commands can autocomplete paths, for example if there's a directory in **/c/myVeryLongPathname** and we're currently in **/c**:

```
$ pwd
/c
$ cd myV<PRESS TAB>
$ cd myVeryLongPathname/ <-- auto completed
```

To navigate up one level from a directory you can reference the special ".." (two dots) directory:

```
$ pwd
/c/dir
$ cd ..
$ pwd
/c
```

Note there's a space between **cd** and the two dots.

Using ODX

Now that we know how to navigate around directories using the **cd** command, place some images in a directory of your choice (e.g. **D:\book\projects\test\images** or **/home/user/projects/test/images**).

We can then start processing the images with ODX by typing:

Windows:

```
(odx) C:\ODX> run d:\book\projects\test [options]
```

macOS/Linux:

```
$ docker run -ti --rm -v /home/user/projects/test:/datasets/code
 ↪  webodm/odx --project-path /datasets [options]
```

In place of **[options]** you can add any of the task options we've covered in the Task Options in Depth chapter. For example, to change the orthophoto resolution, generate a DSM and restart a task from the MVS step, we can add:

```
--orthophoto-resolution 2 --dsm --rerun-from openmvs
```

If you forget what options are available, you can append `--help` to the command.

If the docker commands above looks ominous, don't worry. The next chapter contains a more in-depth discussion of docker.

Throughout this book I mostly use command line examples that invoke docker. On Windows, equivalent commands are achieved by removing the docker specific flags, keeping the ODX options at the end of the command (except `--project-path`) and using `run` instead of `docker`. For example:

```
$ docker run -ti --rm -v /book/projects/test:/datasets/code
↪ webodm/odx --project-path /datasets --orthophoto-resolution
↪ 2
```

On Windows becomes:

```
(odx) C:\ODX> run d:\book\projects\test --orthophoto-resolution
↪ 2
```

Remember to always run Windows commands from the ODX Console.

Processed Files Owned By Root

On Linux and macOS you might notice that once your images are done processing the resulting files cannot be changed or deleted! This is a peculiarity of docker in which the output files are created within the docker container, and since the container runs with a root (admin) user, all files are also owned by root. To get back control of the files, run:

```
$ sudo chown -R $(whoami):$(whoami) /path/to/project
```

You can check who owns a directory by typing:

```
$ ls -al
drwxrwxrwx  2 foo bar 4.0K Jun 10 18:02 images
```

In the output above the **images** directory is owned by the user *foo* and group *bar*.

Add New Processing Nodes to WebODM

On Windows, you can launch a new NodeODX node by first downloading the latest NodeODX Windows binaries from github.com/WebODM/NodeODX/releases. If you have already installed WebODM, these are already available at **C:\WebODM\resources\app\apps\NodeODX**. You can then launch a new node by opening a Command Prompt, navigating to the NodeODX directory and typing:

```
C:\WebODM\resources\app\apps\NodeODX>nodeodx.exe --odx_path
 ↪  ..\ODX -q 1 --token secret
```

Making sure the `odx_path` is a correct path to ODX.

On macOS/Linux you can do the same by typing:

```
docker run --rm -it -p 3000:3000 webodm/nodeodx -q 1 --token
 ↪  secret
```

The command asks docker to launch a new container using the **webodm/nodeodx** image (the latest version of NodeODX), using port 3000, setting a maximum number of concurrent tasks to 1 and protecting the node from unauthorized access using the password *secret*.

From WebODM you can then press the **Add New** button under the **Processing Nodes** menu. For the *hostname/IP* field type the IP of the computer. For the *port* field type *3000*. For the *token* field type *secret*. You can also add an optional *label* for your node. Then press **Save**.

You should now be able to process multiple tasks in parallel using multiple machines.

Examine EXIF/XMP Tags

Sometimes it can be useful to examine which tags are available in an image. Exiftool[1] is one of the best tools to perform this job. You can install exiftool on your local machine or you can also use the copy that's included in ODX.

To list all EXIF/XMP tags in an image, you can run:

```
(odx) C:\ODX> SuperBuild\install\bin\exiftool.exe
↪  C:\book\projects\test\images\DJI_0030.JPG
```

```
docker run -ti --rm --entrypoint
↪  /code/SuperBuild/install/bin/exiftool -v
↪  /book/projects/test:/datasets/test webodm/odx
↪  /datasets/test/images/DJI_0030.JPG
```

To view only the raw XMP tags, append the `-xmp -b` arguments:

[1] Exiftool: exiftool.org/

```
docker run -ti --rm --entrypoint
 ↪  /code/SuperBuild/install/bin/exiftool -v
 ↪  /book/projects/test:/datasets/test webodm/odx
 ↪  /datasets/test/images/DJI_0030.JPG -xmp -b
...
drone-dji:AbsoluteAltitude="+198.61"
drone-dji:RelativeAltitude="+40.10"
drone-dji:GimbalRollDegree="+0.00"
```

Further Readings

While not required for the purpose of using ODX, users interested in expanding their skills with the command line should read the *Learn the Bash Command Line* tutorial available at ryanstutorials.net/linuxtutorial/. It contains a much more comprehensive introduction, including file manipulation, editing, pipes and process management.

On Windows, the *Windows Commands*[2] reference is an in-depth guide for using the command line.

[2]Windows Commands: learn.microsoft.com/en-us/windows-server/administration/windows-commands/windows-commands

16. Docker Essentials

Several WebODM projects make extensive use of Docker as an installation and management tool. If you have ever had to deal with it, you probably know that it's confusing, seems to eat your disk space without reason and will unexpectedly error out with some cryptic message once in a while.

For the good and the bad however, Docker is here to stay. This chapter is here to help you understand its concepts and covers some basic commands as they are applicable to using WebODM projects more efficiently. I encourage readers to follow along and type the commands in a terminal while going through this chapter.

On Windows it's not necessary to use docker, as most WebODM projects can run natively, but it *can* be used. If you're on Windows and you don't want to use docker, you can safely skip this chapter.

Docker Basics

Without getting too technical, docker is a tool that lets people wrap software and all their dependencies into *docker images*. Think of these *images* as programs. Each image can be used to start one or more *containers*. Think of containers as running instances of the program. To make an analogy, if Notepad is a docker image, opening the Notepad program 3 times is the equivalent of running 3 containers.

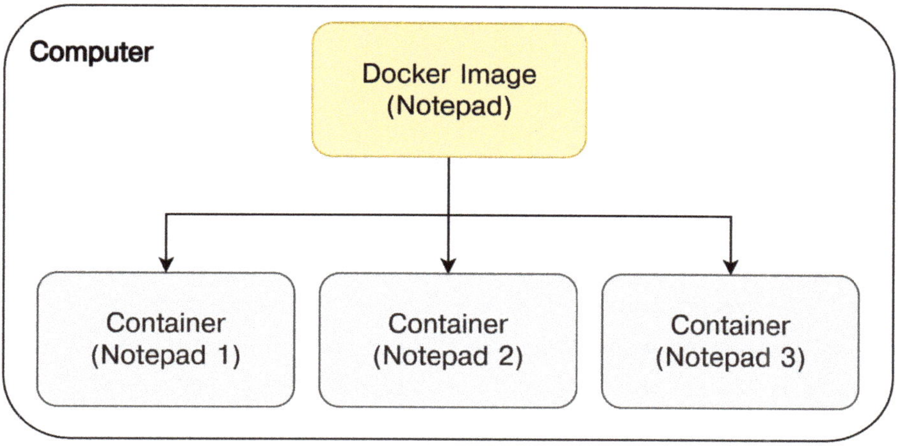

Docker Example

Unlike normal programs however, docker images carry with them the entire operating system from which they are built! Among many other advantages, this allows us to run a program that was built for Linux under a different operating system. Of course there are disadvantages too (extra space, some overhead, etc.), but life is about trade-offs isn't it?

Docker images have names and they follow this convention:

```
username/imagename[:tag]
```

The **:tag** part of the name is optional and when omitted it defaults to **latest**. As an example, let's look at the full command we typically use to start an ODX process:

```
$ docker run -ti --rm -v /book/projects/test:/datasets/code
 ↪ webodm/odx --project-path /datasets
```

We are asking docker to start a new container using the **webodm/odx:latest** image.

- `-ti` (short for `-t -i`) asks docker to create a terminal and to keep it open (even if we close the window). Just remember to use this argument, or no console output will be displayed.
- `--rm` asks to remove the container once it's done (by default containers are not destroyed after they are done, they are left in a *stopped* state).
- `-v` maps a volume (we'll discuss volumes below). Finally, we pass the `--project-path` option to the ODX process inside the container.

The **docker run** command follows this syntax:

```
docker run [docker options] [image name] [program options]
```

Managing Containers

We mentioned earlier that by default containers are not removed. A container begins in a running state and when it's done it switches to a stopped state. Let's see what happens when we forget to pass the `--rm` flag to a run command.

```
$ docker run -ti -v /book/projects/test:/datasets/code
 ↪  webodm/odx --project-path /datasets
```

When the command stops, we list all containers by issuing:

```
$ docker ps -a
CONTAINER ID        IMAGE                                  COMMAND
↪   CREATED             STATUS                             PORTS
↪   NAMES
ab89e4b71b65        webodm/odx                          "python
↪   /code/run.py..."   9 minutes ago        Exited (1) 9 minutes
```

We can see that the **webodm/odx** container was not removed after exiting (because we didn't specify `--rm`). The **ps -a** command shows all containers, whether they are running or are stopped.

Each container has a unique identifier (or *hash*), which can be used to reference the container in other commands. In these examples, the container's hash is **ab89e4b71b65**.

To remove the container we just launched we can type:

```
$ docker rm ab89e4b71b65
```

If there are no conflicting hashes, you can also shorthand the hash by typing just one or more of the hash's beginning characters:

```
$ docker rm ab8
```

If you get the error message *Error response from daemon: You cannot remove a running container*, it's because only containers that are in stopped state can be removed. To stop a container issue:

```
$ docker stop ab8
```

We can verify that the container has been removed by issuing:

```
$ docker ps -a
CONTAINER ID        IMAGE                                COMMAND
↪   CREATED             STATUS                           PORTS
↪   NAMES
```

You should be comfortable creating, listing and removing containers.

Two other important flags for the **run** command are **-d** and **-p:**

```
$ docker run -d -p 3000:3000 webodm/nodeodx
ab89e4b71b65
```

The **-d** flag can be used to start a container in the background. When a container is launched in the background the console does not *attach* to the container but returns immediately with the hash of the created container. This way you can launch multiple containers without having to open new terminal windows. The **-p** flag exposes a network port from the container so that you can access it from the outside:

```
-p <port of computer>:<port inside container>
```

In the example above, the **webodm/nodeodx** image contains a web server that is configured to run on port 3000. By passing **-p 3000:3000** we ask docker to make the web server (running on port 3000 **inside** the container) available on port 3000 on our computer. This might seem confusing, but allows you to do cool things such as:

```
$ docker run -d -p 3000:3000 webodm/nodeodx
$ docker run -d -p 3001:3000 webodm/nodeodx
```

Which launches two separate NodeODX instances on ports 3000 and 3001, respectively.

Managing Images

Docker images can be created from a Dockerfile[1], which is a text file that tells docker how to create a particular image.

You don't necessarily need to build your own images. The WebODM developers have already built and published docker images for everyone to use. You can see what images are available by visiting hub.docker.com/u/webodm.

There are some advantages to building your own images. You can make modifications to the software and in some cases (mostly just for ODX), you can gain a modest speed-up! For example, the public **webodm/odx** image has been built to support a large variety of computers (old and new), so certain optimizations that are available only on newer computers have been disabled. If you have a shiny new computer, building your own image can take advantage of those optimizations. To build your own image of ODX, first download ODX's source code, then navigate to the folder that contains the Dockerfile and type:

```
$ docker build -t myusername/odx .
```

After building it (which will take a while), use **myusername/odx** to run your image:

[1] Dockerfile Reference: docs.docker.com/reference/dockerfile

```
$ docker run --rm -ti [...] myusername/odx [...]
```

The first time you use **docker run**, Docker checks if the image you are requesting already exists on the computer. If it does, docker runs it. If it doesn't, docker attempts to download it from hub.docker.com. You can list the images that exist on your computer by using:

```
$ docker images
REPOSITORY                     TAG                    IMAGE ID
 ↪  CREATED               SIZE
webodm/odx                   latest               f2275dac6ee1
 ↪  22 hours ago           3.14GB
```

Notice that just like containers, every image has a unique identifier (or *hash*) associated with it. With time you might decide that you do not need some images anymore and you can reclaim some disk space by removing older images. For example, let's remove the **webodm/odx** image:

```
$ docker rmi f22
```

When a new image becomes available on hub.docker.com (for example, when a new version of ODX becomes available) you need to manually specify that you'd like to download the new version using the **pull** command:

```
$ docker pull webodm/odx
```

Managing Volumes

Up to this point, we've been using this **run** command quite a bit:

```
$ docker run -ti -v /book/projects/test:/datasets/code
↪  webodm/odx --project-path /datasets
```

But what does the **-v** /book/projects/test**:/datasets/code** part do? It creates a mapped volume:

```
-v <path on computer>:<path in container>
```

Containers are isolated environments. A container has its own internal directory structure, separate from that of the computer that is running the container. If we want to allow the container to access some of the files on our computer, we need to specifically allow it and we need to specify where we want to make our files accessible inside the container.

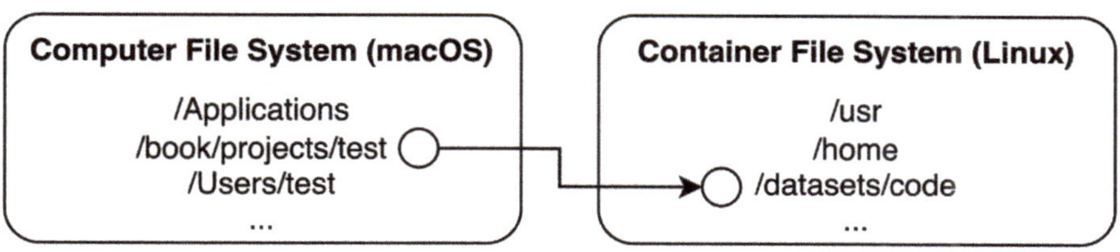

Docker volume mapping. Files in **/book/projects/test** will be available in the container's **/datasets/code** path

If you have ever setup a network drive, you map a network location to a drive so that you can access some path such as **G:\folder**, even though **folder** might be a folder residing on a remote computer. Docker volumes are kind of like network drives, but from your computer to containers.

If this still doesn't make sense, just remember that in order to get files in and out of a container we use mapped volumes.

In our example we took the **/book/projects/test** folder from our computer and made it available in the container's **/datasets/code** directory:

```
Computer --> Container
/book/projects/test/images/1.JPG --> /datasets/code/images/1.JPG
/book/projects/test/images/2.JPG --> /datasets/code/images/2.JPG
```

A quick note on the choice of **/datasets/code** as a path for the ODX container. **/datasets** is an arbitrary path, which we specify via `--project-path /datasets` when running ODX:

```
docker run -ti -v /book/projects/test:/datasets/code webodm/odx
 ↪  --project-path /datasets
```

code is the default *project name*. We can also explicitly specify a different project name and rewrite the command above as:

```
docker run -ti -v /book/projects/test:/datasets/example1
 ↪  webodm/odx --project-path /datasets example1
```

But because developers are lazy (the good kind of lazy) if a project name is omitted it defaults to **code**, so it's shorter to write.

Docker Compose Basics

While docker is used for running individual containers, docker compose is used for running multiple containers. It's helpful to look at WebODM as an example of an application that uses docker compose. WebODM, for example, is made of several components:

- A web application (*webodm/webodm_webapp*)
- A database (*webodm/webodm_db*)
- A message broker (*library/redis*)
- A processing engine (*webodm/nodeodx*)

You can see the parts that make WebODM by looking at the contents of the various **docker-compose*.yml** files from the WebODM source code. These .yml (YAML) files control the behavior of docker compose. In Part II of this book when we launched WebODM via:

```
./webodm.sh start
```

all we did was to start docker compose. In fact *webodm.sh* is mostly an interface to docker compose. It provides a way to coordinate the launch of multiple containers, decide which containers should be launched before others, how storage should be configured and many other features. It's outside the scope of this book to have an exhaustive overview of docker compose, but interested readers can find an exhaustive guide from the docker documentation[2]. I invite you to open **webodm.sh** as well as the various **docker-compose*.yml** files with a text editor to see how they are defined.

Docker compose can combine multiple .yml files together. For example:

```
$ docker-compose -f docker-compose.yml -f
↪  docker-compose.settings.yml up
```

reads the configuration from **docker-compose.yml**, then applies the configuration from **docker-compose.settings.yml**, overriding or extending previous configurations. In this case **docker-compose.settings.yml** (load

[2]Docker compose: docs.docker.com/compose/

additional configuration settings) extends **docker-compose.yml** (just start WebODM, no additional settings). The **up** command asks to create and start all the containers defined in the configurations. Other useful commands include:

Stop the containers (but don't remove them):

```
$ docker compose -f docker-compose.yml stop
```

Stop the containers and remove them:

```
$ docker compose -f docker-compose.yml down
```

Update all images from hub.docker.com:

```
$ docker compose -f docker-compose.yml pull
```

Managing Disk Space

Without the occasional cleaning, over time docker will happily eat up all of your disk space! This can happen when containers have not been removed, when many images have been downloaded, or when stray volumes have been abandoned. Docker is supposedly doing you a favor by not removing things automatically (what if you needed that image you built 3 years ago?). Luckily there's a useful command for cleaning things up:

```
$ docker system prune
```

Changing Entrypoint

Starting and stopping containers can take time. Also when processing fails, it might be difficult to inspect what went wrong. I suggest a two step approach to running ODX datasets with docker:

```
$ docker run -ti -v /book/projects/test:/datasets/example1
 ↪  --entrypoint bash webodm/odx
root@898747d1f3a8:/code# ./run.sh --project-path /datasets
 ↪  example1
root@898747d1f3a8:/code# exit
```

By passing the `--entrypoint bash` flag we ask docker to ignore the default startup command of the container and to run bash (a Linux shell) instead. The # confirms that we are inside the container, running a bash shell. Now we can run the ODX process by invoking *run.sh*. The difference with this approach is that if something fails, we can more easily check for problems and restart the process. To exit the container we type **exit**.

Assigning Names To Containers

When you have lots of containers, nothing is more frustrating than remembering hash IDs. You can assign names when running a container and then reference that name in future commands.

```
$ docker run -d -p 3000:3000 --name mynode webodm/nodeodx
$ docker stop mynode
$ docker rm mynode
```

Jumping Into Existing Containers

Sometimes you'd really like to know what the heck is going on inside a container, without restarting it (you would lose its state). For example, I sometimes wonder if WebODM is really done downloading that long running task that seems to take forever.

```
$ docker ps
CONTAINER ID        IMAGE                                   COMMAND
 ↪  CREATED              STATUS              PORTS
 ↪  NAMES
aff69c390477        webodm/webodm_webapp   "/bin/bash -c
 ↪  'chmod..."   46 hours ago        Up 3 hours
 ↪  0.0.0.0:8000->8000/tcp    webapp

$ docker exec -ti aff69c390477 bash
root@aff69c390477:/webodm# ls
 ↪  app/media/project/<id>/task/<id>/assets
all.zip    images.json    odm_orthophoto/    odm_dem/ ...
```

The **exec** command allows you to execute a command from a running container. In this instance we choose to execute a bash shell, which gives us a command prompt to inspect the contents of the container while it's running!

Docker is a powerful tool, but can also be a bit intimidating. I hope this chapter removed some of the mysteries that surround it, hopefully while sparking some curiosity. While it's not necessary to become a master of docker to use any of the WebODM software, familiarity with it will certainly help. The docker documentation website[3] is a much more comprehensive resource for those wishing to expand their knowledge.

[3] Docker Documentation: docs.docker.com

17. GPU Processing

If your computer has an NVIDIA graphics card and you're on Windows or Linux, the program can use it to speed up some parts of the processing pipeline, specifically during Multi-View Stereo (MVS).

At the time of writing, GPU acceleration is not available on macOS or with other video cards.

The NVIDIA card needs to support compute capability version 3.5 or higher. You can check your card's compute capability version from NVIDIA's website[1].

Windows

On Windows there's nothing to do. The native installation of WebODM/ODX already includes support for NVIDIA GPUs. To verify that the GPU is working correctly, you should be able to see the following line from the task's console output:

```
[INFO] CUDA drivers detected
```

[1] GPU Compute Capability developer.nvidia.com/cuda-gpus

Linux

On Linux we need to explicitly enable GPU support. This is because the default **node-odx-1** processing node is setup from the **webodm/nodeodx:latest** docker image[2] which does not include any of the GPU code.

Before enabling GPU support, we need to setup NVIDIA's drivers and software.

Step 1. Install NVIDIA Container Toolkit

Assuming you have already installed the NVIDIA drivers[3] of your graphics card, you'll need to install the NVIDIA Container Toolkit software.

I recommend to follow the most up-to-date instructions from the NVIDIA Container Toolkit website[4] and if your distribution is not officially supported, to do an internet search for "install nvidia container toolkit on X".

After you have configured docker to recognize the container runtime, you should be able to run this command without errors:

```
$ docker run --rm --runtime=nvidia --gpus all
↪ nvidia/cuda:12.8.2-base-ubuntu24.04 nvidia-smi
```

Step 2. Start WebODM with GPU support

When starting WebODM, pass the `--gpu` argument:

[2]NodeODX docker image: hub.docker.com/r/webodm/nodeodx
[3]NVIDIA drivers: nvidia.com/en-us/drivers/
[4]NVIDIA Container Toolkit's Install Guide: docs.nvidia.com/datacenter/cloud-native/container-toolkit/latest/install-guide.html

```
./webodm.sh restart --gpu
```

That's it! The default **node-odx-1** node will now be GPU enabled. In the background, passing the `--gpu` argument instructs WebODM to use the **webodm/nodeodx:gpu** docker image.

Notes on GPU usage

Using the GPU can dramatically reduce the time it takes to compute the MVS step. Other parts of the pipeline are not GPU-accelerated, which means that it's normal for the GPU to sit idle for long periods of time during processing.

Also, while the GPU code is almost logically equivalent to the CPU code, it's not numerically equivalent, so you will notice that the point clouds computed using the GPU are going to differ slightly compared to CPU runs. If this is a concern, one can disable GPU usage by enabling the no-gpu option.

18. Processing Large Datasets

ODX can require a lot of memory for processing. These memory requirements increase almost proportionally with the number of images and their resolution. Twice the images? Need twice the RAM! Of course at some point you might encounter a very large dataset made of dozens of thousands of images, but don't have 800GB of RAM just lying around.

This is where a nice feature called **split-merge** comes into play. This feature splits a large dataset into smaller, manageable parts called submodels that have some overlap between them. Each submodel is processed independently, either one at a time on a single machine (local split-merge) or in parallel on multiple machines (distributed split-merge). Once all submodels have been processed, the results are merged back together into a single consistent model. With this approach people can process much larger datasets using much less powerful computers. Enabling split-merge changes the ODX execution pipeline:

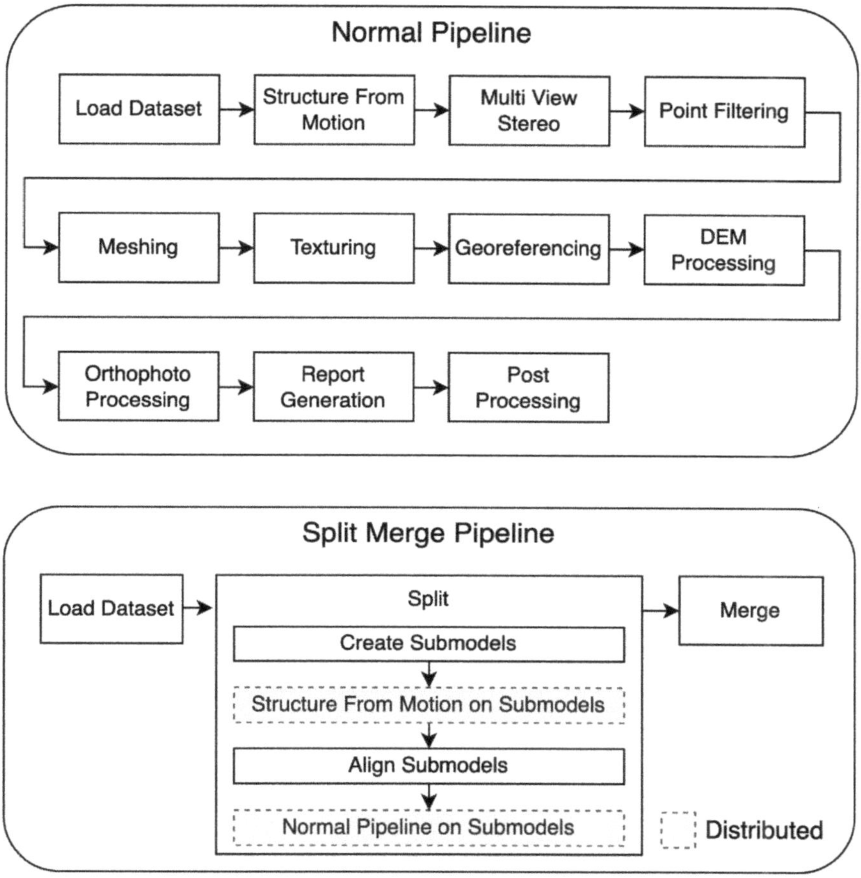

Split-merge pipeline. Step 2 and 4 of the split section can be performed in parallel on separate machines when using distributed split-merge

Split-Merge Options

split

Split-merge can be used either from the command line (ODX) or from WebODM and is enabled by setting the **split** option. Split-merge will be turned on anytime the number of images is less than the value specified in the option. For example, a dataset with 300 images and split set to 150 will turn on split-merge.

This option specifies the **average** number of images that should be included in each submodel. Note that this does not guarantee that your submodels will have this exact amount of images. In fact, some submodels might end up having twice as many images as others. It just means that the sum of all submodel images divided by the number of submodels will be approximately equal to the split value.

split-overlap

In order to align and merge results, each submodel must be reconstructed with a certain amount of overlap and redundancy with other submodels.

Overlap area between two submodels

The amount of overlap in meters is specified with this option. Datasets captured at higher altitudes should use a larger value, while those captured at lower altitudes can use lower values. More overlap will significantly slow down computation because of the redundancy of processed data, but can help achieve better model alignment during the merge step. If the resulting DEMs and point clouds from different submodels show big gaps in elevation, try increasing the overlap.

sm-cluster

This option enables distributed split-merge by specifying a URL to a ClusterODX instance. The process of setting up ClusterODX is described later in the Distributed Split-Merge section of this chapter.

merge

After splitting and computing each individual submodel, results need to be merged back together. By default all supported outputs (point clouds, DEMs and orthophotos) are merged. A user can use this option to specify that only a particular type of output should be merged. Valid options are:

- all
- pointcloud
- orthophoto
- dem

Local Split-Merge

To use local split-merge pass the **split** and **split-overlap** options:

```
$ docker run -ti --rm -v /book/projects/test:/datasets/code
↪  webodm/odx --project-path /datasets --split 100
↪  --split-overlap 75
```

In the example above, submodels will be stored in **/book/projects/test/submodels** while the merged results will be stored in the usual folders.

Each submodel folder (**submodels/submodel_xxxx**) is itself a valid ODX project. So if a submodel fails to process, you can re-run the individual submodel to isolate potential issues by running:

```
$ docker run -ti --rm -v /book/projects/test:/datasets/code
↪ webodm/odx --project-path /datasets/code/submodels
↪ --orthophoto-cutline --dem-euclidean-map submodel_xxxx
```

The orthophoto-cutline and dem-euclidean-map options are always required for the purpose of merging DEMs and orthophotos. If an error occurs while processing one of the submodels, the process will stop. After fixing the problem, one can resume the process by re-running the initial command:

```
$ docker run -ti --rm -v /book/projects/test:/datasets/code
↪ webodm/odx --project-path /datasets --split 100
↪ --split-overlap 75
```

Submodels that correctly processed the first time will **not** be re-processed, unless the **rerun-from split** option is passed. Execution will resume from the failed submodel.

If a task fails at the merge step, after all submodels have finished processing, you can check for issues and resume the merge step by typing:

```
$ docker run -ti --rm -v /book/projects/test:/datasets/code
↪ webodm/odx --project-path /datasets --split 100
↪ --split-overlap 75 --rerun merge --merge all
```

Distributed Split-Merge

Distributed split-merge works just like local split-merge, but can be much faster, as submodels are processed independently in parallel by many machines. All that is required is to setup an instance of ClusterODX and link some NodeODX nodes to it.

ClusterODX

ClusterODX is a program to connect together NodeODX API compatible nodes. It allows for tasks to be distributed across multiple nodes while taking into consideration factors such as maximum number of images, queue size and slot availability. It can also automatically spin up/down nodes based on demand using several cloud computing providers such as Digital Ocean, AWS and Hetzner.

ClusterODX looks like a normal NodeODX node from the outside and can operate with any tool that also works with NodeODX. To start ClusterODX on macOS/Linux, type:

```
$ git clone https://github.com/WebODM/ClusterODX
$ cd ClusterODX
$ docker compose up
```

On Windows you can download pre-built binaries from https://github.com/WebODM/ClusterODX/releases. Extract them in a folder of your choice, then double-click `clusterodx.exe`.

If you open your browser to http://localhost:10000 you should be greeted with:

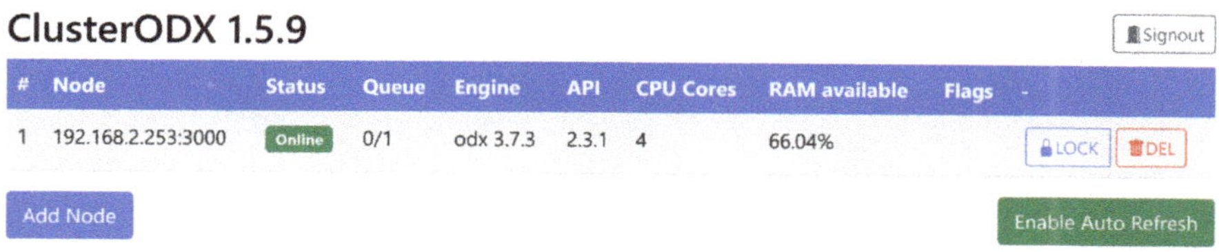

ClusterODX web admin page

Let's add some nodes to ClusterODX. If you have another computer with docker installed, you can run:

```
$ docker run -d -p 3000:3000 webodm/nodeodx
```

which will launch a new instance of NodeODX on port 3000. Now it's time to connect our new NodeODX node to ClusterODX.

Click the **Add Node** button from ClusterODX's web admin page, set the **Hostname** field to the IP address or hostname of the computer running NodeODX, set the **Port** to 3000 and press **Apply**.

Note: if the node queue displays a strange *0/99999999999* value, you probably added ClusterODX to itself, which can happen if you used **localhost** as a hostname and are running ClusterODX using docker. This is probably not what you wanted, so find the actual IP address of the machine running NodeODX, delete the erroneous node and re-add the correct one.

To verify that things are working you can now open http://localhost:4000. If things are working you should see the NodeODX web interface. This means ClusterODX is properly forwarding requests to the NodeODX nodes.

Managing ClusterODX

A lot of functions in ClusterODX are not available from the web interface and are instead accessible via an archaic but functional protocol called **telnet.** On Linux and macOS telnet is usually installed by default (if it isn't, Google how to install it). On Windows you usually need to enable it. From an elevated shell (right-click **Command Prompt** and select **Run As Administrator**) type:

```
$ pkgmgr /iu:"TelnetClient"
```

Then restart the shell. Once **telnet** is available, type:

```
$ telnet localhost 8080
Connected to ...
Escape character is '^]'.
#
```

Typing **HELP** will show you all available commands. To add a NodeODX node use the **NODE ADD** command:

```
# NODE ADD ipofmachine 3000
# NODE LIST
2) ipofmachine:3000 [online] [0/2] <version 2.2.2>
```

You'll need to change **ipofmachine** with the IP address or hostname of the computer running NodeODX.

You can connect as many nodes as you want to ClusterODX. If you have a variety of computers, some more powerful than others, you can start NodeODX instances with the **max_images** option:

```
$ docker run -d -p 3000:3000 webodm/nodeodx --max_images 300
```

This way NodeODX will be instructed to process datasets only up to 300 images. ClusterODX will take this factor into consideration when processing new tasks and will forward the task to the first machine capable of handling it.

A useful command is **NODE LOCK** which will prevent a certain node from being used by ClusterODX:

```
# NODE LOCK 1
# NODE LIST
1) ipofmachine:3000 [online] [0/2] <version 2.2.2> [L]
```

In the setup above, all tasks will be forwarded to machine 2. Nodes that are locked can be unlocked with **NODE UNLOCK**.

ClusterODX can also use cloud computing providers such as Digital Ocean to spin up/down computing instances on demand. Check the ClusterODX README[1] for the latest instructions on how to configure it.

Distributed Run

Now that ClusterODX is setup, running distributed split-merge is the same as running local split-merge, except that we pass an additional sm-cluster option that specifies the URL to a ClusterODX instance.

```
$ docker run -ti --rm -v /book/projects/test:/datasets/code
↪  webodm/odx --project-path /datasets --split 100
↪  --split-overlap 75 --sm-cluster http://ipofclusterodx:4000
```

[1]ClusterODX: github.com/WebODM/ClusterODX

Note that if you are running this command on the same machine as ClusterODX, **ipofclusterodx** cannot be **localhost**, because **localhost** refers to the **webodm/odx** container and not your machine. To find out the correct IP address, run:

```
$ docker ps
CONTAINER ID        IMAGE                                   COMMAND
 ↪  CREATED               STATUS                  PORTS
 ↪  NAMES
5a86a35fe643        webodm/clusterodx
 ↪  "/usr/bin/nodejs /va..."   4 days ago          Up 2 hours
 ↪  0.0.0.0:4000->3000/tcp   node-odm-1

$ docker inspect -f "{{range
 ↪  .NetworkSettings.Networks}}{{.IPAddress}}{{end}}" 5a86
172.23.0.5
```

and use that IP instead. In the example above, we can then use `--sm-cluster http://172.23.0.5:4000`.

On Windows, check with the command `ipconfig /all` the exact IP address of your computer running ClusterODX.

Using Image Groups and GCPs

You can control how a dataset should be split by placing an **image_groups.txt** file in your project folder. For example, if your images are in **D:\book\projects\test\images**, you can create a **D:\book\projects\test\image_groups.txt** file with the following content:

```
1.JPG A
```

```
2.JPG A
3.JPG B
4.JPG B
5.JPG C
[...]
```

where the items on the left are image names and items on the right represent submodel groups. If you run out of letters use *AA*, *BB*, etc. The file is case-sensitive so uppercase and lowercase letters are treated differently.

If this file is detected during split-merge, the **split** value will be ignored and the dataset will be split according to the rules specified in the **image_groups.txt** file. You will still need to pass **split** to enable the split-merge workflow.

In WebODM, the **image_groups.txt** file can be uploaded along with the images when creating a task and will be automatically used.

Image groups are important when using GCPs. GCPs can be used with split-merge, but care should be exercised to make sure there are at least 3 GCPs that fall within each submodel. If less than 3 GCPs are present in a submodel, the submodel will be aligned with the GPS information from EXIF data and by looking at the position of other submodels, but won't be as accurate.

You can use GCPs with split-merge just like you would use GCPs for a normal run.

Limitations

With split-merge you get point clouds, DEMs and orthophotos, but not 3D textured meshes or PDF reports. You can still access the individual 3D textured meshes from each submodel, but no *global* 3D textured mesh or report is generated.

All of the problems listed in the Camera Calibration chapter are magnified when using split-merge. It's imperative to follow best practices for data acquisition.

While the longest parts of processing can be parallelized in distributed split-merge, a dataset still needs to be split, aligned and merged on a single machine. The merge step in particular, for really large datasets, could still make the machine run out of memory. Choose **orthophoto-resolution**, **dem-resolution** and **pc-quality** parameters conservatively. Use the most powerful machine you have available to start a distributed split-merge task.

19. The NodeODX API

ODX is a processing engine and WebODM is a friendly user interface. NodeODX[1] was historically built to allow WebODM to communicate with ODX over a network. Today NodeODX has expanded its role and is the glue that binds together many WebODM projects. Each project understands the API that NodeODX defines. When we say *NodeODX* we are referring to the reference implementation of the NodeODX API available at github.com/WebODM/NodeODX.

At its core, the API defines ways to easily create new tasks, manage such tasks (cancel, delete, restart), download results and query status information.

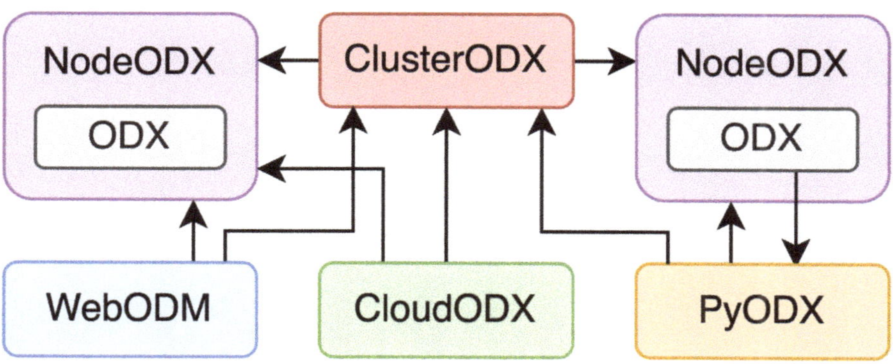

Many WebODM projects use the NodeODX API to communicate with each other

[1]Node is a reference to Node.js, the language NodeODX is written in

In this chapter we'll learn to manually launch a NodeODX instance, explore its web interface and do some manual interaction with the API using cURL, a program that allows us to make web requests. Familiarity with the NodeODX API can give users a better understanding of the network interactions that happen between the various projects.

The API has different versions and is mostly backward compatible with previous implementations whenever a new version is released. The most up-to-date specification is available online[2], while a copy of the latest specification at the time of writing is reported for reference at the end of this chapter.

Launching a NodeODX Instance

Starting NodeODX can be done by running:

```
$ docker run -d -p 3000:3000 webodm/nodeodx
```

Opening a web browser to localhost:3000 loads the NodeODX interface. The interface is minimal by design as it doesn't try to compete with the more advanced functionalities of WebODM. It's mostly a test bed for accessing the API functions.

[2] NodeODX spec: github.com/WebODM/NodeODX/blob/master/docs/index.adoc

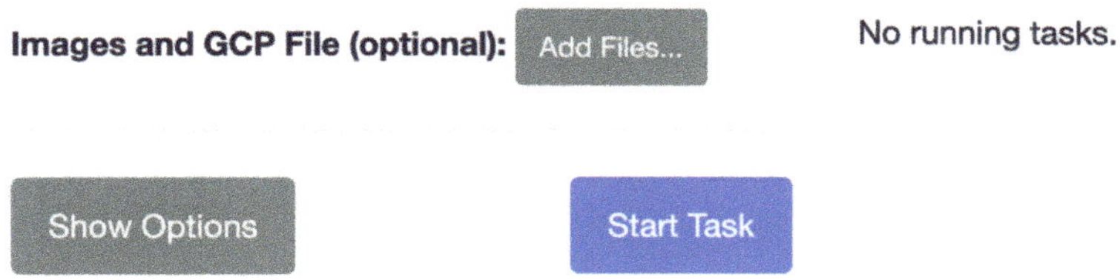

NodeODX's user interface

From the web interface you can upload images, set task options, monitor and manage tasks, retrieve console outputs and download results. Not all functions of the API are exposed through the web interface, but most are.

NodeODX Configuration

You can pass several options while launching NodeODX. The full list is available by running:

```
$ docker run --rm -ti webodm/nodeodx --help
Usage: node index.js [options]
```

On Windows, if you have installed WebODM natively, from a Command Prompt you can use:

```
C:\WebODM\resources\app\apps\NodeODX>nodeodx --odx_path ..\ODX
↪ --help
```

Below you can find the most important ones:

Option	Description	Default
`-p, --port <number>`	Port to bind the server to, or "auto" to automatically find an available port	3000
`--odx_path <path>`	Path to ODM's code	/code
`-q <number>`	Number of simultaneous processing tasks	2
`--cleanup_tasks_after <number>`	Number of minutes that elapse before deleting finished and canceled tasks	2800
`--test`	Enable test mode. In test mode, no commands are sent to ODX. This can be useful during development or testing	false
`--token <token>`	Sets a token that needs to be passed with every request. This can be used to limit access to the node only to token holders	none
`--max_images <number>`	Specify the maximum number of images that this processing node supports	none
`--webhook <url>`	Specify a POST URL endpoint to be invoked when a task completes processing	none

Option	Description	Default
`--max_concurrency <number>`	Place a cap on the max-concurrency option to use for each task	no limit
`--max_runtime <number>`	Number of minutes (approximate) that a task is allowed to run before being forcibly canceled (timeout)	no limit

Using the API with cURL

In the following examples we will use the curl program to interact directly with the API to upload some images, query task status and download results. Curl can be downloaded for any platform from curl.haxx.se/download.html.

There's almost no practical reason for using curl to interact with NodeODX, aside from the learning experience and for the occasional troubleshooting. If you need to process tasks with NodeODX from the command line, CloudODX[3] is probably a much better tool for the job.

But since we are learning, curl will be used here.

Create a New Task

If you have some images in **/book/projects/test/images** you can run:

```
$ pwd
/book/projects/test
```

[3]CloudODX: github.com/WebODM/CloudODX

```
$ curl -F images=@images/DJI_0018.JPG -F
 ↪  images=@images/DJI_0019.JPG -F name=Test -X POST
 ↪  http://localhost:3000/task/new
{"uuid":"d3b2-48d2-adfb-6c8e14e4"}
```

You can use more images by adding more **-F images** parameters.

With this command we created a new task and named it *Test*. The *name* field was passed via a FormData parameter. Some API functions accept parameters via query and body parameters also. We'll look at examples of both later. The API communicates via a format called JSON[4]. JSON is a nice format because both machines and humans can read it. For example, if an error occurs, the program will output:

```
{"error": "description of the error"}
```

In the case of a successful call to **/task/new** we received back the task ID (identifier) that was created.

Query Task Information

After a task is created, we can query its status by referencing its ID using **/task/<uuid>/info**:

```
$ curl http://localhost:3000/task/d3b2-48d2-adfb-6c8e14e4/info
{"uuid":"d3b2-48d2-adfb-6c8e14e4","name":"Test",
"dateCreated":1560702697082, ...
```

[4]JavaScript Object Notation (JSON): json.org

We can also display the entire task output by invoking:

```
$ curl http://localhost:3000/task/d3b2-48d2-adfb-6c8e14e4/output
↪
["[INFO] Initializing ODX 3.7.3 - Fri Apr 08 13:02:13
↪  2026","[INFO] ==============", ...
```

Or use the optional **?line=** query parameter to retrieve the last 2 lines of output:

```
$ curl
↪  http://localhost:3000/task/d3b2-48d2-adfb-6c8e14e4/output?line=-2
["[INFO] Writing exif overrides","[INFO] Maximum photo
↪  dimensions: 1280px"]
```

Query parameters are passed directly via URLs.

So far we saw examples of passing query and FormData parameters. Next we'll look at passing body parameters.

Remove a Task

We can invoke **/task/delete** to delete a task:

```
$ curl -d uuid=d3b2-48d2-adfb-6c8e14e4
↪  http://localhost:3000/task/remove
{"success":true}
```

Note the task ID is passed via a *uuid* body parameter.

API Specification

The content below is a technical reference. If you're not interested in the nitty gritty details of the NodeODX API you can skip this section.

Version : 2.3.1

GET /auth/info

Description

Retrieves login information for this node.

Responses

HTTP Code	Description
200	Login Information

Login Information

Name	Description
loginUrl	URL (absolute or relative) where to make a POST request to obtain a token, or null if login is disabled.
message	Message to be displayed to the user prior to login/registration. This might include instructions on how to register or login, or to communicate that authentication is not available.

Name	Description
registerUrl	URL (absolute or relative) where to make a POST request to register a user, or null if registration is disabled.

POST /auth/login

Description

Retrieve a token from a username/password pair.

Parameters

Type	Name	Description
Body	**password**	Password
Body	**username**	Username

Responses

HTTP Code	Description
200	Login Succeeded
default	Error

Login Succeeded

Name	Description
token	Token to be passed as a query parameter to other API calls.

POST /auth/register

Description

Register a new username/password.

Parameters

Type	Name	Description
Body	**password**	Password
Body	**username**	Username

Responses

HTTP Code	Description
200	Response

GET /info

Description

Retrieves information about this node

Parameters

Type	Name	Description
Query	**token** *optional*	Token required for authentication (when authentication is required).

Responses

HTTP Code	Description
200	Info

Info

Name	Description
availableMemory *optional*	Amount of RAM available in bytes
cpuCores *optional*	Number of CPU cores (virtual)
engine	Lowercase identifier of processing engine

Name	Description
engineVersion	Current version of processing engine
maxImages	Maximum number of images allowed for new tasks or null if there's no limit.
maxParallelTasks *optional*	Maximum number of tasks that can be processed simultaneously
taskQueueCount	Number of tasks currently being processed or waiting to be processed
totalMemory *optional*	Amount of total RAM in the system in bytes
version	Current API version

GET /options

Description

Retrieves the command line options that can be passed to process a task

Parameters

Type	Name	Description
Query	**token** *optional*	Token required for authentication (when authentication is required).

Responses

HTTP Code	Description
200	Options

Option

Name	Description
domain	Valid range of values (for example, “positive integer” or “float > 0.0”)
help	Description of what this option does
name	Command line option (exactly as it is passed to the ODX process, minus the leading ‘–’)
type	Datatype of the value of this option
value	Default value of this option

POST /task/cancel

Description

Cancels a task (stops its execution, or prevents it from being executed)

Parameters

Type	Name	Description
Query	**token** *optional*	Token required for authentication (when authentication is required).
Body	**uuid**	UUID of the task

Responses

HTTP Code	Description
200	Command Received

GET /task/list

Description

Gets the list of tasks available on this node.

Parameters

Type	Name	Description
Query	**token** *optional*	Token required for authentication (when authentication is required).

Responses

HTTP Code	Description
200	Task List
default	Error

Task List

Name	Description
uuid	UUID of the task

POST /task/new

Description

Creates a new task and places it at the end of the processing queue. For uploading really large tasks, see /task/new/init instead.

Parameters

Type	Name	Description
Header	**set-uuid** *optional*	An optional UUID string that will be used as UUID for this task instead of generating a random one.

Type	Name	Description
Query	**token** *optional*	Token required for authentication (when authentication is required).
FormData	**dateCreated** *optional*	An optional timestamp overriding the default creation date of the task.
FormData	**images** *optional*	Images to process, plus optional files such as a GEO file (geo.txt), image groups file (image_groups.txt), GCP file (*.txt), seed file (seed.zip) or alignment files (align.las, align.laz, align.tif). If included, the GCP file should have .txt extension. If included, the seed archive pre-populates the task directory with its contents.
FormData	**name** *optional*	An optional name to be associated with the task
FormData	**options** *optional*	Serialized JSON string of the options to use for processing, as an array of the format: [{name: option1, value: value1}, {name: option2, value: value2}, ...]. For example, [{"name":"min-num-features","value":"5000"}]. For a list of all options, call /options
FormData	**outputs** *optional*	An optional serialized JSON string of paths relative to the project directory that should be included in the all.zip result file, overriding the default behavior.

Type	Name	Description
FormData	**skipPostProcessing** *optional*	When set, skips generation of point cloud tiles.
FormData	**webhook** *optional*	Optional URL to call when processing has ended (either successfully or unsuccessfully).
FormData	**zipurl** *optional*	URL of the zip file containing the images to process, plus an optional GEO file and/or an optional GCP file. If included, the GCP file should have .txt extension

Responses

HTTP Code	Description
200	Success
default	Error

Success

Name	Description
uuid	UUID of the newly created task

Consumes

- `multipart/form-data`

POST /task/new/commit/{uuid}

Description

Creates a new task for which images have been uploaded via /task/new/upload.

Parameters

Type	Name	Description
Path	**uuid**	UUID of the task
Query	**token** *optional*	Token required for authentication (when authentication is required).

Responses

HTTP Code	Description
200	Success
default	Error

Success

Name	Description
uuid	UUID of the newly created task

POST /task/new/init

Description

Initialize the upload of a new task. If successful, a user can start uploading files via /task/new/upload. The task will not start until /task/new/commit is called.

Parameters

Type	Name	Description
Header	**set-uuid** *optional*	An optional UUID string that will be used as UUID for this task instead of generating a random one.
Query	**token** *optional*	Token required for authentication (when authentication is required).
FormData	**dateCreated** *optional*	An optional timestamp overriding the default creation date of the task.
FormData	**name** *optional*	An optional name to be associated with the task
FormData	**options** *optional*	Serialized JSON string of the options to use for processing, as an array of the format: [{name: option1, value: value1}, {name: option2, value: value2}, ...]. For example, [{"name":"min-num-features","value":"5000"}]. For a list of all options, call /options

Type	Name	Description
FormData	**outputs** *optional*	An optional serialized JSON string of paths relative to the project directory that should be included in the all.zip result file, overriding the default behavior.
FormData	**skipPostProcessing** *optional*	When set, skips generation of point cloud tiles.
FormData	**webhook** *optional*	Optional URL to call when processing has ended (either successfully or unsuccessfully).

Responses

HTTP Code	Description
200	Success
default	Error

Success

Name	Description
uuid	UUID of the newly created task

POST /task/new/upload/{uuid}

Description

Adds one or more files to the task created via /task/new/init. It does not start the task. To start the task, call /task/new/commit.

Parameters

Type	Name	Description
Path	**uuid**	UUID of the task
Query	**token** *optional*	Token required for authentication (when authentication is required).
FormData	**images**	Images to process, plus optional files such as a GEO file (geo.txt), image groups file (image_groups.txt), GCP file (*.txt), seed file (seed.zip) or alignment files (align.las, align.laz, align.tif). If included, the GCP file should have .txt extension. If included, the seed archive pre-polulates the task directory with its contents.

Responses

HTTP Code	Description
200	File Received
default	Error

Consumes

- `multipart/form-data`

POST /task/remove

Description

Removes a task and deletes all of its assets

Parameters

Type	Name	Description
Query	**token** *optional*	Token required for authentication (when authentication is required).
Body	**uuid**	UUID of the task

Responses

HTTP Code	Description
200	Command Received

POST /task/restart

Description

Restarts a task that was previously canceled, that had failed to process or that successfully completed

Parameters

Type	Name	Description
Query	**token** *optional*	Token required for authentication (when authentication is required).
Body	**options** *optional*	Serialized JSON string of the options to use for processing, as an array of the format: [{name: option1, value: value1}, {name: option2, value: value2}, ...]. For example, [{"name":"min-num-features","value":"5000"}]. For a list of all options, call /options. Overrides the previous options set for this task.
Body	**uuid**	UUID of the task

Responses

HTTP Code	Description
200	Command Received

GET /task/{uuid}/download/{asset}

Description

Retrieves an asset (the output of ODX's processing) associated with a task

Parameters

Type	Name	Description
Path	**asset**	Type of asset to download. Use "all.zip" for zip file containing all assets.
Path	**uuid**	UUID of the task
Query	**token** *optional*	Token required for authentication (when authentication is required).

Responses

HTTP Code	Description
200	Asset File
default	Error message

Produces

- `application/zip`

GET /task/{uuid}/info

Description

Gets information about this task, such as name, creation date, processing time, status, command line options and number of images being processed. See schema definition for a full list.

Parameters

Type	Name	Description
Path	**uuid**	UUID of the task
Query	**token** *optional*	Token required for authentication (when authentication is required).
Query	**with_output** *optional*	Optionally retrieve the console output for this task. The parameter specifies the line number that the console output should be truncated from. For example, passing a value of 100 will retrieve the console output starting from line 100. By default no console output is added to the response.

Responses

HTTP Code	Description
200	Task Information
default	Error

Task Information

Name	Description
dateCreated	Timestamp
imagesCount	Number of images
name	Task name
options	List of options used to process this task
output *optional*	Console output for the task (only if requested via ?output=N)
processingTime	Milliseconds that have elapsed since the task started being processed.
status	Status code
uuid	UUID

options

Name	Description
name	Option name (example: “mesh-octree-depth”)
value	Value (example: 9)

status

Name	Description
code	Status code (10 = QUEUED, 20 = RUNNING, 30 = FAILED, 40 = COMPLETED, 50 = CANCELED)

GET /task/{uuid}/output

Description

Retrieves the console output of the ODX process. Useful for monitoring execution and to provide updates to the user.

Parameters

Type	Name	Description
Path	**uuid**	UUID of the task

Type	Name	Description
Query	**line** *optional*	Optional line number that the console output should be truncated from. For example, passing a value of 100 will retrieve the console output starting from line 100. Defaults to 0 (retrieve all console output)
Query	**token** *optional*	Token required for authentication (when authentication is required).

Responses

HTTP Code	Description
200	Console Output
default	Error

Definitions

Error

Name	Description
error	Description of the error

Response

Name	Description
error *optional*	Error message if an error occurred
success	true if the command succeeded, false otherwise

Exercises

Armed with your new knowledge, read the NodeODX specification document and try to perform the following tasks:

- The API defines two ways to create new tasks. We've already used **/task/new**, which is a simplified method that uploads all images at once. NodeODX also exposes a chunked API for uploading images in parallel. Using **/task/new/init**, **/task/new/upload** and **/task/new/commit**, can you create a task using them?
- JSON can be used to specify task options. For example, to set the processing option **orthophoto-resolution** we first encode it to JSON [{"name":"orthophoto-resolution","value":"2"}] then, we can pass it to the *options* FormData parameter of **/task/new**. Search Google for information on the JSON format and how to use arrays. Afterwards, can you find a way to pass multiple options to **/task/new**?
- Can you restart NodeODX with the **token** parameter to add an authentication token and then invoke any of the API functions using the **?token=** Query parameter in the URLs? What happens if you forget to pass the token to your URLs?

If you get stuck, ask for help to the WebODM community[5].

[5] WebODM Community: webodm.org/community

20. Automated Processing With Python

What's better than aerial data processing? Automated aerial data processing of course!

In The NodeODX API chapter we've learned how to use the NodeODX API by using cURL. Now we will learn about PyODX, a Python library for communicating with the NodeODX API. Python is a programming language that is used by many WebODM projects and is popular language in the geospatial community. This chapter will not try to teach the fundamentals of Python, as there are already plenty of free online resources for that[1]. Previous knowledge of Python is preferred, but not required. Python is a very descriptive language and readers should be able to follow the examples even without formal training in Python.

Why would you want to use Python (instead of cURL or CloudODX)? With Python you can leverage the image processing capabilities of ODX to create new, custom applications that have an aerial image processing component. For example, you could build:

- A platform for counting trees using modern computer vision techniques after a user uploads drone images.

[1]Python for Beginners: python.org/about/gettingstarted/

- An application that detects when SD cards are inserted in a computer and automatically processes images without user interaction.
- An application for downloading video segments from YouTube and automatically generating 3D reconstructions from scenes of your favorite movies.

Obviously each of these applications can be complex and requires coding skills, but PyODX would help you with the image processing part of the implementation.

It should be noted that PyODX does a bit more than a simply communicating with NodeODX, as it deals with things such as managing parallel downloads (a sort of download accelerator which makes network transfers faster), parallel uploads, automatic retries for fault tolerance, as well as dealing with backward-compatibility issues between API versions.

Getting Started

On Windows Python can be installed by visiting python.org, is already preinstalled on macOS and can be installed on Linux via package management systems. Just make sure to install a 3.x version (and not a 2.x version, which is outdated).

After Python is installed, verify that you are on 3.x:

```
$ python --version
Python 3.14.5
```

After that, you can install PyODX by running:

```
$ pip install -U pyodx
```

For the rest of the chapter, we'll assume there's already a NodeODX instance running on `localhost:3000`

You can use any text editor you want to write Python code. I prefer to use the free and open source Visual Studio Code[2] but any text editor will do. All examples below are also available for download from github.com/uav4geo/webodm-book-assets.

Example 1: Hello NodeODX

Type the following program into a new file using your text editor, then save it as **hello.py**.

```
from pyodx import Node, exceptions

node = Node('localhost', 3000)
try:
    print(node.info())
except exceptions.NodeConnectionError as e:
    print("Cannot connect: " + str(e))
```

Then run it:

```
$ python hello.py
{'version': '2.3.1', 'task_queue_count': 0, ...}
```

[2]Visual Studio Code: code.visualstudio.com/

We have successfully retrieved the NodeODX instance information. We also check for any connection errors just in case we have forgotten to launch the NodeODX instance and print an error message if we can't connect to the node.

There are a few different types of errors (*exceptions* in Python jargon) that we can handle:

- **GenericError**: A generic catch-all exception related to anything PyODX
- **NodeServerError**: The server replied in a manner which we did not expect. Usually this indicates a temporary malfunction of the node
- **NodeConnectionError**: A connection problem (such as a timeout or a network error) has occurred
- **NodeResponseError**: The node responded with an error message indicating that the requested operation failed
- **TaskFailedError**: A task did not complete successfully
- **RangeNotAvailableError**: A download attempt to use Range requests failed

Example 2: Process Datasets

For this example, save it as **process.py** and place the file in the same folder where some aerial images are stored (e.g. **D:\book\projects\test\images**):

```
import glob
from pyodx import Node, exceptions

node = Node("localhost", 3000)

try:
    # Get all JPG files in directory
```

```
    images = glob.glob("*.JPG") + glob.glob("*.jpg") + glob.glob("*.JPEG") + glob.glob("*.jpeg")

    print("Uploading images...")
    task = node.create_task(images, {'dsm': True, 'orthophoto-resolution': 2})
    print(task.info())

    try:
        def print_status(task_info):
            msecs = task_info.processing_time
            seconds = int((msecs / 1000) % 60)
            minutes = int((msecs / (1000 * 60)) % 60)
            hours = int((msecs / (1000 * 60 * 60)) % 24)
            print("Task is running: %02d:%02d:%02d" % (hours, minutes, seconds), end="\r")
        task.wait_for_completion(status_callback=print_status)

        print("Task completed, downloading results...")

        # Retrieve results
        def print_download(progress):
            print("Download: %s%%" % progress, end="\r")
        task.download_assets("./results", progress_callback=print_download)

        print("Assets saved in ./results")
    except exceptions.TaskFailedError as e:
        print("\n".join(task.output()))

except exceptions.NodeConnectionError as e:
    print("Cannot connect: %s" % e)
```

```
except exceptions.GenericError as e:
    print("Error: %s" % e)
```

Then run it via:

```
python process.py
Uploading images...
{'uuid': '9dfcc56a-806f-4c78-9bd3-2ba0005037ce', 'name': 'Task
 ↪  of 2023-06-06T06:14:19.948Z', 'date_created':
 ↪  datetime.datetime(2023, 6, 6, 6, 14, 19), 'processing_time':
 ↪  4, 'status': <TaskStatus.RUNNING: 20>, 'last_error': '',
 ↪  'options': [{'name': 'dsm', 'value': True}, {'name':
 ↪  'orthophoto-resolution', 'value': 2}, {'name': 'pc-ept',
 ↪  'value': True}, {'name': 'cog', 'value': True}, {'name':
 ↪  'gltf', 'value': True}], 'images_count': 18, 'progress': 0,
 ↪  'output': []}
Task completed, downloading results...
Assets saved in ./results
```

This is a more comprehensive example. First, we create a **Node** instance. From that instance we can create new tasks via **create_task()** which take as input a list of image paths (which we generate via the **glob** function) and returns a **Task** instance. We then wait for the results to be ready via **wait_for_completion()** and we ask to be notified of status updates by displaying how long the task has been running for. If a task fails at any point in time, **wait_for_completion()** raises a **TaskFailerError.** We "catch" that error and display the task output to the user if that happens. When the task completes, we download the results and display download progress information.

Concluding Remarks

PyODX is a simple module that makes it straightforward to leverage the capabilities of ODX with Python. It's also a module used within ODX itself and WebODM and will continue to be well supported in the future. If you need to use NodeODX with a different programming language, you can use PyODX as a reference to write a client for your language of choice.

API Reference

The following reference is from PyODX version 1.5.14 (the latest version as of the writing of this book). The reference to the latest version can be found online at pyodx.webodm.org

class pyodx.api.Node(host, port, token='', timeout=30)

A client to interact with the NodeODX API.

Parameters:

- **host** (*str*) – Hostname or IP address of processing node
- **port** (*int*) – Port of processing node
- **token** (*str*) – token to use for authentication
- **timeout** (*int*) – timeout value in seconds for network requests

create_task(*files, options{}, name=None, progress_callback=None, skip_post_processing=False, webhook=None, outputs=[], parallel_uploads=10, max_retries=5, retry_timeout=5*)

Start processing a new task. At a minimum you need to pass a list of image paths. All other parameters are optional. Parameters:

- **files** (*list*) – list of image paths + optional GCP file path.
- **options** (*dict*) – options to use, for example {'orthophoto-resolution': 3, ...}
- **name** (*str*) – name for the task
- **progress_callback** (*function*) – callback reporting upload progress percentage
- **skip_post_processing** (*bool*) – When true, skips generation of map tiles, derivate assets, point cloud tiles.
- **webhook** (*str*) – Optional URL to call when processing has ended (either successfully or unsuccessfully).
- **outputs** (*list*) – Optional paths relative to the project directory that should be included in the all.zip result file, overriding the default behavior.
- **parallel_uploads** (*int*) – Number of parallel uploads.
- **max_retries** (*int*) – Number of attempts to make before giving up on a file upload.
- **retry_timeout** (*int*) – Wait at least these many seconds before attempting to upload a file a second time, multiplied by the retry number.

Returns: **Task()**

static **from_url**(*url, timeout=30*)

Create a Node instance from a URL.

```
n = Node.from_url("http://localhost:3000?token=abc")
```

Parameters:

- **url** (*str*) – URL in the format proto://hostname:port/?token=value

- **timeout** (*int*) – timeout value in seconds for network requests

Returns: **Node()**

get_task(*uuid*)

Helper method to initialize a task from an existing UUID Parameters:

uuid – Unique identifier of the task

info()

Retrieve information about this node

Returns: **NodeInfo()**

options()

Retrieve the options available for creating new tasks on this node.

Returns: [**NodeOption()**]

url(*url, query={}*)

Get a URL relative to this node. Parameters:

- **url** (*str*) – relative URL
- **query** (*dict*) – query values to append to the URL

Returns: Absolute URL (str)

version_greater_or_equal_than(*version*)

Checks whether this node version is greater than or equal than a certain version number Parameters:

version (*str*) – version number to compare

Returns: bool

class pyodx.api.Task(node, uuid)

A task is created to process images. To create a task, use **create_task()**.
Parameters:

- **node** (**Node()**) – node this task belongs to
- **uuid** (*str*) – Unique identifier assigned to this task.

cancel()

Cancel this task.

Returns: task was canceled or not (bool)

download_assets(*destination, progress_callback=None, parallel_downloads=16, parallel_chunks_size=10*)

Download this task's assets to a directory. Parameters:

- **destination** (*str*) – directory where to download assets. If the directory does not exist, it will be created.
- **progress_callback** (*function*) – an optional callback with one parameter, the download progress percentage
- **parallel_downloads** (*int*) – maximum number of parallel downloads if the node supports http range.
- **parallel_chunks_size** (*int*) – size in MB of chunks for parallel downloads

Returns: path to saved assets (str)

download_zip(*destination, progress_callback=None, parallel_downloads=16, parallel_chunks_size=10*)

Download this task's assets archive to a directory. Parameters:

- **destination** (*str*) – directory where to download assets archive. If the directory does not exist, it will be created.

- **progress_callback** (*function*) – an optional callback with one parameter, the download progress percentage.
- **parallel_downloads** (*int*) – maximum number of parallel downloads if the node supports http range.
- **parallel_chunks_size** (*int*) – size in MB of chunks for parallel downloads

Returns: path to .zip archive file (str)

info(*with_output=None*)

Retrieves information about this task.

Returns: **TaskInfo()**

output(*line=0*)

Retrieve console task output. Parameters:

line (*int*) – Optional line number that the console output should be truncated from. For example, passing a value of 100 will retrieve the console output starting from line 100. Negative numbers are also allowed. For example -50 will retrieve the last 50 lines of console output. Defaults to 0 (retrieve all console output).

Returns: console output (one list item per row) ([str])

remove()

Remove this task.

Returns: task was removed or not (bool)

restart(*options=None*)

Restart this task. Parameters:

options (*dict*) – options to use, for example {'orthophoto-resolution': 3, ...}

Returns: task was restarted or not (bool)

wait_for_completion(*status_callback=None, interval=3, max_retries=5, retry_timeout=5*)

Wait for the task to complete. The call will block until the task status has become **COMPLETED()**. If the status is set to **CANCELED()** or **FAILED()** it raises a TaskFailedError exception. Parameters:

- **status_callback** (*function*) – optional callback that will be called with task info updates every interval seconds.
- **interval** (*int*) – seconds between status checks.
- **max_retries** (*int*) – number of repeated attempts that should be made to receive a status update before giving up.
- **retry_timeout** (*int*) – wait N*retry_timeout between attempts, where N is the attempt number.

class pyodx.types.NodeInfo(json)

Information about a node Parameters:

- **version** (*str*) – Current API version
- **task_queue_count** (*int*) – Number of tasks currently being processed or waiting to be processed
- **total_memory** (*int*) – Amount of total RAM in the system in bytes
- **available_memory** (*int*) – Amount of RAM available in bytes
- **cpu_cores** (*int*) – Number of virtual CPU cores
- **max_images** (*int*) – Maximum number of images allowed for new tasks or None if there's no limit.
- **max_parallel_tasks** (*int*) – Maximum number of tasks that can be processed simultaneously
- **odm_version** (*str*) – (deprecated, use engine_version instead)
- **engine** (*str*) – Lowercase identifier of the engine (odm, micmac, ...)

- **engine_version** (*str*) – Current engine version

class pyodx.types.NodeOption(domain, help, name, value, type)

A node option available to be passed to a node. Parameters:

- **domain** (*str*) – Valid range of values
- **help** (*str*) – Description of what this option does
- **name** (*str*) – Option name
- **value** (*str*) – Default value for this option
- **type** (*str*) – One of: ['int', 'float', 'string', 'bool', 'enum']

class pyodx.types.TaskInfo(json)

Task information Parameters:

- **uuid** (*str*) – Unique identifier
- **name** (*str*) – Human friendly name
- **date_created** (*datetime*) – Creation date and time
- **processing_time** (*int*) – Milliseconds that have elapsed since the start of processing, or -1 if no information is available.
- **status** (**pyodx.types.TaskStatus()**) – status (running, queued, etc.)
- **last_error** (*str*) – if the task fails, this will be set to a string representing the last error that occurred, otherwise it's an empty string.
- **options** (*dict*) – options used for this task
- **images_count** (*int*) – Number of images (+ GCP file)
- **progress** (*float*) – Percentage progress (estimated) of the task
- **output** (*[str]*) – Optional console output (one list item per row). This is populated only if the with_output parameter is passed to info().

class pyodx.types.TaskStatus

Task status Parameters:

- **QUEUED** – Task's files have been uploaded and are waiting to be processed.
- **RUNNING** – Task is currently being processed.
- **FAILED** – Task has failed for some reason (not enough images, out of memory, etc.
- **COMPLETED** – Task has completed. Assets are be ready to be downloaded.
- **CANCELED** – Task was manually canceled by the user.

Glossary

2.5D Model: A model where elevation is simply *extruded* from the ground plane and thus is not a true 3D model.

Artifacts: undesired alterations generated as the result of a digital process.

API: Application Programming Interface. A set of functions allowing the creation of applications that access the features or data of another application.

Bundle Adjustment: a refinement step during the Structure From Motion process that improves the location of cameras, the 3D points of the scene and the camera parameters.

CloudODX: A command line tool to process aerial imagery in the cloud.

ClusterODX: A NodeODX API compatible autoscalable load balancer and task tracker for connecting multiple NodeODX nodes under a single network address.

CRS: Coordinate Reference System. A CRS is a coordinate-based system used to locate geographical entities.

CSV: Comma Separated Value is a textual file format where fields are typically separated by commas or some other character such as a space or a tab.

cURL: a software providing a library and command-line tool for transferring data using many protocols.

DEM: Digital Elevation Model (either a DSM or a DTM).

Depthmap: An image containing distance information for objects in a scene relative to the camera plane.

Docker: a tool used to launch *containers*, lightweight standalone packages of software. WebODM can use docker to run many of its software. Docker is also the name of the company that develops the tool.

DSM: Digital Surface Model. A 2D representation of elevation that includes terrain, buildings, trees and other structures.

DTM: Digital Terrain Model. A 2D representation of elevation that includes terrain only.

EXIF: Exchangeable Image File Format. A file format for images and their auxiliary tags. EXIF tags are pieces of information embedded within an image. They can include information such as camera model, GPS location of where the image was shot, focal length information and many more.

GCP: Ground Control Point. A GCP is a position measurement made on the ground, often taken at the location of a clearly identifiable marker, to increase the georeferencing accuracy of a reconstruction.

GSD: Ground Sampling Distance. In an aerial photo, it's the distance between pixels measured on the ground.

Mesh: A collection of vertices, edges and faces that define the shape of a 3D model. A mesh does not include color information such as textures.

MVS: Multi-View Stereo is a branch of study in computer vision that focuses on the reconstruction of 3D models from multiple overlapping image pairs. MVS programs expect that information about cameras has already been computed.

NodeODX: A lightweight REST API to access photogrammetry engines such as ODX, MicMac and LGT.

Noise: An unwanted interference. When applied to point clouds, it indicates points that should not be present or that were missed during outlier filtering.

Nadir: The direction pointing directly below a particular location.

ODX: A photogrammetry engine to generate maps, point clouds, 3D models and DEMs from aerial and ground images.

OpenSfM: Open source structure from Motion library written in Python. The library serves as a processing pipeline for reconstructing camera poses and 3D scenes from multiple images.

Orthophoto: An image that has been *orthorectified*, warped in such a way that distances and scales are uniform.

Photogrammetry: the process of obtaining reliable information about physical objects and the environment through the process of using photographic images.

Preemptive Matching: During the Structure From Motion process, the act of reducing the possible number of pair candidates by using the location information stored in the EXIF tags of the images.

PyODX: A Python SDK for adding aerial image processing capabilities to applications.

RTK: Real Time Kinematics. A satellite navigation technique used to enhance the precision of position data derived from satellite-based positioning systems.

SDK: Software Development Kit. A set of libraries, tools and examples that help software developers to build software with a particular technology.

SFM: Structure From Motion is a photogrammetry technique for estimating 3D objects (structures) from overlapping image sequences (from motion).

Texturing: The act of creating 2D images suitable for use on 3D models, also known as *texture maps* or *texture skins*. Textures give 3D models a realistic appearance.

UAV: Unmanned Aerial Vehicle. An aircraft piloted by remote control or on-board computers.

UI: User Interface.

UTM: Universal Transverse Mercator is a coordinate reference system. It ignores altitude and treats the earth as a perfect ellipsoid.

VM: Virtual Machine. A software program or operating system that works like a separate computer.

WebODM: User-friendly, commercial-grade software for processing aerial imagery.

About The Author

Piero Toffanin is a software developer currently focused on AI, geospatial and drone software development. He has been working on open source software for over 28 years. He's the creator of WebODM and frequently speaks at conferences about drones, geospatial and open source.

https://piero.dev

https://uav4geo.com

www.ingramcontent.com/pod-product-compliance
Lightning Source LLC
LaVergne TN
LVHW050908210926
848482LV00012B/377

* 9 7 9 8 2 3 4 0 9 0 0 1 0 *